BONSAI

■ Step by step to growing success ■

Dave Pike

CROWOOD GARDENING GUIDES

First published in 1989 by
The Crowood Press Ltd
Gipsy Lane, Swindon
Wiltshire SN2 6DQ

British Library Cataloguing in Publication Data

Pike, Dave
    Bonsai: step by step guide to growing success
    1. Bonsai. Cultivation, Manuals
    I. Title
    635.9'772

ISBN 1 85223 128 9

Photographs by Dave Pike
Line illustrations by Claire Upsdale-Jones
English bonsai pots kindly loaned by David Jones

Typeset by Consort Art Graphics, Exeter, Devon
Printed and bound by
Times Publishing Group, Singapore.

Contents

Introduction

This book is written with the beginner in mind, but at the same time I aim to provide a book which will see them through the first ten years of bonsai growing and then be used as a reference for future bonsai practices. To get the best from the book it would be advisable to read through chapter by chapter, as the book has been written for the beginner to follow step by step, and only by reading through the book first will the reader see the complete pattern of bonsai growing.

The first part of the book deals with soils or, as they are termed throughout the book, compost. The beginner may find it tedious to learn all the different types of compost and fertilisers, but without some knowledge, he will soon run into problems. With regard to propagation, I have included both growing on a small scale and growing seedlings on a larger scale. I have found once you start to grow the odd seedling it soon develops into a full scale commitment, utilising the garden coldframe and soil planting area, which can be used for winter storage. I have tried to keep technical terms to a minimum, but it is advisable to try to learn some botanical names.

GOOD AND BAD BONSAI

Although it is nice to grow your own bonsai, and great satisfaction can be gained from doing so, there comes a stage when you are tempted to purchase a semi-mature, commercially grown bonsai, something to look at and admire whilst building the character of your own bonsai seedling. Because of the increase in interest during the last ten years, growers are finding it very hard to meet the demands from garden centres and the general public, especially around the Christmas period. There are a few traders who move into the bonsai business at certain times of the year, picking up supplies of trees from wherever they can find them. Some of the trees are indeed true bonsai, but some are no more than small conifers or shrubs placed in a pot, most without any form of bonsai training. Some of them do look like bonsai, but a pot and a piece of wire placed on a few branches will not make a bonsai.

BONSAI CENTRES

Today there are many good, well-established bonsai centres with people who have spent many years developing and promoting the art of bonsai. The prices are basically comparable, and all follow a general rule of conduct set by governing bodies who represent bonsai for their country or part of the world. Most of the centres offer some form of training in the form of classes or are linked with a local bonsai club. Such training is sometimes offered through the adult education system, and I myself run a ten week course for beginners followed by five weeks at an advanced level.

There are many children taking an interest in bonsai, and for those classed as 'minors' I would advise supervision when using pruning tools, spraying equipment and chemicals.

CHAPTER 1

Bonsai Basics

Many beautiful things in the world today are created from skills which were either born with us or handed down from elders. Creations such as art and music both rely on the senses of sight, feelings and touch. Bonsai involves all three senses, and inspires peace and tranquillity. The word 'bonsai' means a plant in a pot or dish; in Japan they grow not only trees, but also shrubs and herbaceous plants by such methods. In the western world we tend to look on the word 'bonsai' as referring solely to a tree grown in a pot. In fact, only in the last thirty five years have people started to recognise and accept shrubs as bonsai material. Shrubs such as cotoneaster, berberis, chaenomeles and many more can be found in England. The confusion arises when people think that they have to use a dwarfed variety to produce a bonsai tree. I would agree that it helps, but bonsai is a mechanical process, not a genetic one. This mechanical process does occur naturally in different ways, such as a tree growing over a rocky surface which restricts its root growth; the wind bending and twisting the trunk into abstract shapes; sun and drought; and animals feeding on the tops and sides of the plant – all play a part in stunting the tree's growth. We in the bonsai world create similar conditions but take a more tender approach, using a soil with good drainage, and balancing feeding, watering and skilful pruning.

Bonsai first began in China in the Tsin area around the third century BC, then found its way across to Japan in the twelfth century. Because of its links with the Far East, bonsai has always been surrounded by a mystical air, to such an extent that even the trained horticulturists turned away from bonsai, leaving the art to those with bonsai skills handed down to them by past generations. I was lucky to have both a good horticultural background and a love for growing bonsai. Combining the two has given me many years of pleasure producing these small but normal trees in the way they did many centuries ago. In the following pages I will try to take away the air of mystery surrounding bonsai growing and

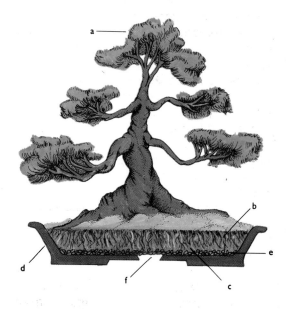

Fig 1   The basic rules of bonsai. (a) Pinching out the top growth. (b) Cutting the roots. (c) Free-draining soil with careful watering and feeding. (d) Shallow pot. (e) Gravel to help drainage. (f) Adequate drainage hole.

5

pass on my basic horticultural skills, combined with years of growing, showing and teaching bonsai. For those who have spent many years developing their own bonsai collection, I hope you too will benefit from the horticultural techniques explained in this book.

SHAPES AND STYLES

There are many shapes and styles connected with bonsai growing. At this stage, the beginner should only use four or five basic shapes. To learn a multitude of styles and Japanese names such as Shakan, Sokan, Yose-Ue would probably take up more time than growing your bonsai. Therefore, it is only necessary to learn such things if you intend following the authentic Japanese customs, but to help those who do wish to learn such names I have listed them below. With all due respect to the Japanese, I have written this book on the trees and styles found in the western part of the globe. Who knows, one day bonsai may be the only way to keep a tree in our concrete planet.

INDOOR AND OUTDOOR

There are two kinds of bonsai, indoor and outdoor, the outdoor being the hardier of the two. In the outdoor category are trees such as maple, oak, elm, beech and most other trees found on English soil. In the indoor category are trees such as the pomegranate, baobab and acacia, from warmer countries. I cover both these sections in more detail in chapters 6 and 7.

POTS

A bonsai pot can come in a variety of shapes, colours and sizes. The materials used in the pots from Japan should tolerate low temperatures, but it can cost up to £100 for a large, high-class pot. The majority of English pots tend to crack in frost conditions, their drainage holes are too large and most are glazed inside. However, there are a few firms in England producing good pots, such as the ones shown in Fig 3. I would stress the importance of *not* using pots which are glazed

JAPANESE NAME	STYLE
Bonkei	Landscapes.
Bunjingi	Tree at an angle with top growth only.
Chok-kan	Formal upright.
Fukinagashi	Windswept.
Han-kengai	Semi-cascade.
Hokidachi	'Broom' shape.
Ikadabuki	Groups in straight line, often called a 'raft'.
Kabudachi	Trees around one root.
Kengai	Cascade.
Literati	Tree at an angle with top growth only.
Neagari	Exposed root system.
Sekijoju	Root over a rock.
Shakan	Slanting trunk.
So-kan	Split trunk.
Moyogi	Informal upright.

Fig 2   Japanese bonsai pots.

Fig 3   English pots.

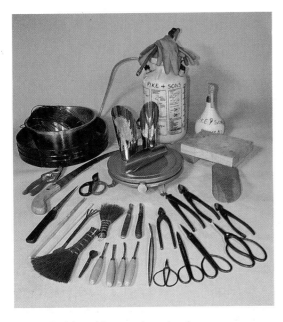

Fig 4   English and Japanese bonsai tools.

inside; they are unsuitable for bonsai, and many people, myself included, have lost trees grown in such pots.

To avoid confusion between pots, trays and dishes, I have listed below all three and their uses:

Pot   Has depth and can be any shape.
Dish   A shallow form of the pot, used mainly for group plantings and bonsai with shallow root systems. Ideal for displaying a good surface root system.
Tray   Not to be confused with a seed tray, it is a long, flat dish without drainage holes and is used as a humidity tray. Another use would be to place a piece of rock, with a bonsai planted into it, in the centre of the tray and then fill it with water to give the illusion of a river or sea.

Fig 4(a)   Pots which are glazed on the inside like this one should not be used for bonsai. Such a pot may cause damage to the root system.

Fig 4(b)   An old Japanese white pine in a rectangular pot.

CHAPTER 2

Soil

The beginner will come across many soil formulas when first starting bonsai growing, many of which have been tried and tested by people who have grown bonsai for a number of years. These are fine for the advanced bonsai grower, and there is no reason why the beginner should not learn a few of the soil techniques from the advanced student, but the materials are not always available and individual trees will need their own pH levels.

The advanced student will talk on soil, mentioning such names as 'Kuro-tsuchi' (a black loam), 'Aka-tsuchi' (a red clay) and 'Tenjin River Sand' (a form of granite), or the 'Kiryu sand' produced from volcanic rock. However, it is far better initially to follow the basic horticultural practices used by most commercial bonsai growers. I would agree that producing the ideal organic soil for your bonsai will make all the difference to the health of the tree, but be patient and learn to understand the tree and its needs; this may take you several years.

You may also be advised to use leaf mould, pine needles and other organic substances, but I would add a word of warning; unless the ingredient has been recommended by an advanced student who has the living proof in the form of a tree, do not use it. Untold damage may be caused through the release of nitrogen, toxic substances or pest and disease from these ingredients, and the grower should proceed with caution. However, once again there is no reason why the beginner should not try and test organic substances on practice material first.

Grading soil is an old practice used by the Japanese to sort soil into large, medium and small particles, by sieving through three different-sized sieves. This was done to allow for good drainage, but the beginner would have difficulty finding the right *type* of loam, clay and sand, and the complexities of particles breaking down under watering and weather conditions must also be understood. Modern bonsai growers still use different size particles, but will use modern material readily found in garden centres. Therefore, experiment with the compost discussed on the following pages until such time as you have found a compost that is ideally suited to your own individual tree.

The soil used for growing your bonsai should be open, allowing air and water to pass through freely, but at the same time having adequate water retention. By this I mean that your soil should have a balance of loam to give the soil body, peat to hold the water and sand to help drainage, assisting the air passage through the soil and generally helping with the physical condition of the soil. Fig 5 shows how the soil particles look in an open soil. Note the large spaces in between each particle which allows air and water to pass freely through the soil. The large soil particle to the left of the diagram shows the film of water around the particle. This is where the tree starts to take in moisture through its root hairs.

The soil used for bonsai should be free from pests and diseases. Soil taken from the garden should not be used unless partially sterilised first.

The term 'sterilising' would mean, in its true

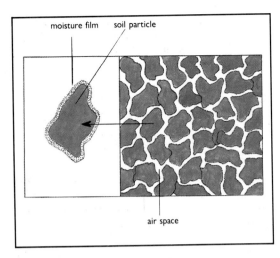

moisture film   soil particle

air space

Fig 5   Air flow and good drainage is a very important consideration when mixing a bonsai compost.

sense, a barren soil, totally without life and completely unsuitable for a tree's existence. Partially sterilising a soil by heat or chemical will, however, free the soil of harmful organisms only. Therefore, by using a compost as shown later in the book, you will save yourself the time and trouble of partially sterilising your soil.

SAND

The sand or sand and gravel used in bonsai must be free of lime. Never use builder's sand, as it has a high lime content. It is important, therefore, always to buy your sand from a garden centre and to make sure that it is labelled 'washed horticultural sand or gravel'.

LOAM

I have already mentioned the term loam. Most soils (or composts as they will be termed from now on) sold in garden centres are loam-free, that is to say they contain peat and plant nutrients. They are much lighter and do not

have as much body as a compost *with* loam. For this reason they are not suitable for bonsai. A soil that contains loam gives you the heaviness to hold the tree in its pot, whereas a tree planted in a loamless compost would need wiring into its pot.

To produce a loam, turf is stacked upside-down in layers with decomposed straw or animal bedding lying between each layer. This is left for about six to seven months, a long and costly process, and one of the reasons why there are so many loamless composts on the market. Before trying to make your own loam, remember that the process takes a long time and you will need to add lime yourself to balance the pH to about 6.3, and the end product will need sterilising. Therefore, it is far better to purchase one of the composts containing loam from your local garden centre.

COMPOST

The materials used in making a compost containing loam are peat, sand and loam, sterilised so that it is free from pest and diseases, to which a balance of plant nutrients are then added. To use a ready-made compost on its own would not be suitable for bonsai. You will see later, for instance, that some trees like an open, sandy compost and some do not. Bonsai trees' individual needs vary, and therefore the compost purchased should only be used as a base to which more sand or peat is then added.

As in all things, there is good and bad, and garden compost is no exception. In some of the bags you may find wood, paper and stones which must be removed by sieving the compost before using it. On each bag of compost you will find a number from one to three; there is also a compost especially for seed. The higher the number, the greater the fertiliser content becomes. I have found I get the best results by using a seed compost or a number one compost and then adding more feed at a later stage.

LEAF MOULD

Leaves are broken down through composting (stacking in layers and allowing them to rot down to form a humus) and are sometimes added to a bonsai compost to give it more body. The type of leaves used will determine how variable in quality the humus is. I have found that leaves from hawthorn and beech are the best to use. If you do add leaf mould to your soil, make sure it has been partially sterilised before using it.

PEAT

There are two types of peat, moss peat, which is light brown in colour and looks like flakes of tobacco, and a black, sooty peat which can turn to a dust when dry. Always use the moss peat. It will cost more, but has the heaviness we need in our bonsai compost.

COMPOST MIXTURES

There are five 'types' of compost: seed, cutting, seedling, open sandy, medium and heavy. Fresh compost containing loam should be purchased from your local garden centre.

Code I (Seed compost) 80 per cent seed compost, 10 per cent moss peat, 10 per cent sharp sand. Sieve seed compost and moss peat. There are also volcanic substances available from local garden centres which are suitable for seed growing.

Code 2 (Cutting compost) 50 per cent moss peat and 50 per cent sharp sand. Sieve moss peat. As with seed compost, there are volcanic substances suitable for cuttings.

Code 3 (Open, sandy compost) 60 per cent seed compost containing loam, 20 per cent moss peat and 20 per cent sharp sand. Sieve seed compost and moss peat.

Code 4 (Medium compost) 70 per cent seed compost containing loam, 15 per cent moss peat and 15 per cent sharp sand. Sieve seed compost and moss peat.

Code 5 (Heavy compost) 80 per cent seed compost containing loam, 10 per cent moss peat and 10 per cent sharp sand. Sieve seed compost and moss peat.

NOTE Grade the compost containing loam with a 1.5mm sieve to remove very fine particles and keep any particles over this size, then grade the moss peat with a 5mm sieve. Mix the two piles together and sieve the combined mixture once more through a 5mm sieve. Sharp sand is then added to the combined mixture (do not grade the sand).

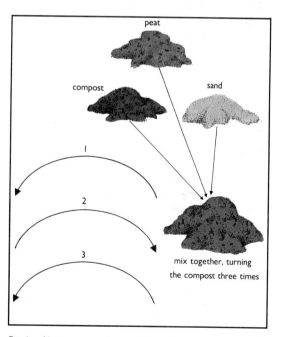

Fig 6   Always use a clean surface when mixing your compost.

Compost Mixing

You must mix compost in a clean area. This can be a large wooden board or a clean area of concrete. Measure your materials of moss peat, sand, compost containing loam and leaf mould (if used) and place them in a pile next to each other on the clean surface. Start by mixing the materials together, and once they are in one heap, turn them over as shown in Fig 6.

The compost should be turned at least three times to allow all the particles to mix together. Small amounts of water can be added if the compost is too dry, mainly to keep down the dust and help the particles to stick together. You should end up with a compost that feels gritty, but at the same time silky, and it should flow easily through your fingers.

FEEDING

Feeding is very important when growing a bonsai. Although we are trying to slow down the rate of growth in our tree, in real terms we are only talking of height and therefore we still wish to produce a thick trunk, with branches which are proportionately balanced to the thickness of that trunk. Essential nutrients which help to produce such a healthy, well balanced growth are fed to the tree through-out its growing season. These essential nutrients are divided into two types, major elements and trace elements.

Major Elements

The first three major elements are carbon, hydrogen and oxygen. Carbon is found in the air which passes through the compost and around the tree, hydrogen can be found in the water which is applied to the compost daily during the growing season, and oxygen is found in both water and air. Therefore, by providing the bonsai with a compost which allows air and water to pass through freely, you are providing the plant with the first three major elements.

The three letters N.P.K. stand for nitrogen, phosphorus and potassium, which are the next three major elements and are applied by feeding.

The bonsai tree will use nitrogen for most of its major growth processes; nitrogen also helps to give the tree its green colour by assisting in the formation of chlorophyll (the green colouring-matter found in plants). Care should be taken not to over-feed your bonsai with nitrogen as this will produce weak, sappy growth, which could be damaged by cold weather, strong winds and pests.

Phosphorus plays an important role in the formation of cells in the young bonsai, particularly in the root. It may seem strange to encourage the roots to grow when most of the time we are trying to control them, but it is very important that the tree maintains a good, strong, healthy root system to help it through a strenuous training programme during the coming seasons.

Potassium will help your bonsai through the cold winter spells, by controlling sap movement and building up the tree's resistance to disease.

N.P.K. is widely known by most bonsai growers as comprising of major elements; however calcium, magnesium and sulphur also play their part in the health of your bonsai tree. Calcium helps in the formation of cells and strengthens the tree's structure, developing the growing tips of the tree and its roots. As with nitrogen, magnesium helps to form chlorophyll and works with phosphorus, which in turn assists in seed formation. One of the main causes of yellow leaves is magnesium deficiency, a term which we call 'chlorosis'. Sulphur is used in protein formation and helps the production of oils in the tree.

Fig 6(a) *Serissa showing signs of deficiency in its foliage (chlorosis).*

Fig 6(b) *As shown in this maple leaf, disfigurations can be caused by weather problems as well as by feeding deficiencies.*

Trace Elements

The bonsai tree will only require small amounts of trace elements such as iron, copper, boron, zinc, manganese and molybdenum. These trace elements work closely with other major elements by speeding up the chemical reactions taking place inside the tree.

Iron and manganese both help with the formation of chlorophyll, and a deficiency will cause yellowing of the leaves (chlorosis). Boron works with calcium to strengthen the tree's structure; a deficiency will reduce the plant's resistance to disease.

All of the chemical fertilisers used should contain both major and trace elements. Be sure to read the packet carefully when purchasing it from your local garden centre.

FEEDING PROGRAMME

In the list below I give three feeding changes to cover the period of the growing season, one for spring, one for summer and one for autumn. By combining them with a compost which is low in nutrients you will have more control over the growth rate during the growing season.

IMPORTANT Always read the instructions given on the box, bottle, or packet. Never over-feed your tree – if the growth is too slow and you are working to a feeding programme, do not be tempted to add more feed, as this can result in root damage and soil contamination. Always use a clean watering-can or sprayer, and never use the same container from which you have used weedkiller, insecticide, or cleaning fluid. Finally, always wash out your container after feeding, then wash your hands with clean water.

Feeding Programme for Hardy and Indoor Bonsai

	April/May/June	July/August	September/October
N	7	10	tomato feed
P	7	12	tomato feed
K	7	14	tomato feed
	(plus trace elements)	(plus trace elements)	(plus trace elements)

CHAPTER 3

Seed Collection and Propagation

There is no such thing as bonsai seeds, only seeds which are suitable for bonsai. Many people think seeds from bonsai trees will reproduce bonsai trees; in fact they will grow into normal-size trees if left unattended. There are two ways of obtaining your bonsai seed; collecting from the wild, or buying from your local garden centre.

When collecting from the wild, there are two points to remember. Firstly, always ask for permission before collecting from woods, parks or private gardens. Secondly, seeds taken from varieties, cultivars and hybrid trees will not always grow true to form. This means that if a tree is crossed to produce a variegated leaf and you collect the seed from this tree, it will have a mix of variegated, part-variegated and non-variegated seedlings. Therefore, it will be found that only species which are true wild trees will come true when grown from seed. To produce a tree identical to the original, or to 'clone' as we term it, you would need to grow it from a cutting and *not* a seed.

The time to collect the seed depends on the type of tree or shrub, and when it flowers. Shrubs such as cotoneaster and pyracantha have small white flowers, and chaenomeles have large, colourful blooms, but not all tree flowers are recognised *as* flowers. You will find that most tree and shrub seeds are ready from late summer to autumn.

It is very important to collect the seeds before they go into their dormancy, the period in which nature sets a protective layer around the seeds and holds them back until the conditions are right for germination. The seeds should therefore be gathered before they start to ripen.

STRATIFICATION

If the seeds have started their dormancy period, you will need to stratify them. This is a process used to overcome dormancy, and to do this you will need a seed tray and horticultural sand. The amounts of materials used in the process are one part seed to three parts sand. Mix the two together and fill a seed tray that has a depth of 7.5cm (3in) and drainage holes at the bottom. Alternatively, as shown in Fig 7, spread a 2.5cm (1in) layer of the peat–sand mixture over the bottom of the seed tray, then place a layer of seeds on top and cover with a second 2.5cm (1in) layer of the mixture, followed by a second layer of seed and so on until you have filled the seed tray.

Now place the seed tray in the refrigerator with a temperature between 1–4°C (30–40°F) for a period of four to six weeks, or place them outside in the coldest part of the garden, north-facing if possible. Out of the two I prefer the outside placement, basically because of the rise and fall in temperature which tends to have more effect on the seed coat.

The period for leaving the seeds outside depends on the seed being stratified. Seeds

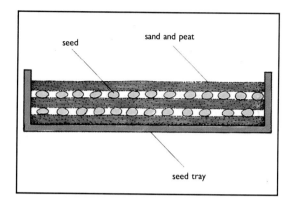

Fig 7 To stratify the seeds place them in the fridge or the coldest part of the garden during the winter.

such as berberis, cotoneaster, Chinese juniper, crab apple, cherry and pyracantha, all need a period of five to six months. Some seeds will not store or over-winter, such as the seeds of the horse chestnut and oak, which are collected green and sown in September or October.

PACKET SEEDS

Not many garden centres stock tree seeds; it will therefore be necessary to order from a seed specialist, or bonsai nursery, by mail order. When you receive the seeds, check on the packet for the current date and make sure the seeds are fresh. Inside you should find instructions telling you what to do with them. You will probably find the seeds have been classed as hard, medium or soft, depending on the type you ordered. Most of the packets will only contain the common name, so in the list below I have used common names only.

Hard seeds Oak, elm, horse chestnut, crab apple, beech and maple.

Medium seeds Southern beech, bamboo, ginkgo, mulberry, wisteria, tree of heaven, pagoda tree, wattle and Christ's Thorn.

Soft seeds Acacia, Bo tree, kaffir, monkey puzzle, octopus tree, pomegranate and yellow shower tree.

SOWING SEEDS

There are two types of seed, one which will need the heat and protection of a glasshouse and one which is a hardier seed and can be sown outside. On pages 18 to 19 you will find a list telling you the type of seed, where to sow it and when.

INDOOR SEEDS

Indoor seeds are sown in a seed tray and placed in a glasshouse, propagator or cold-frame with heating cables (see pages 22 to 25). The temperature for general seed sowing should be 12–18°C (54–64°F), but some of the exotic trees such as baobab may need a slightly higher temperature.

Step one Always use a clean seed tray, with plenty of drainage holes in the bottom.

Step two Fill the seed tray to just over half way with a seed compost, similar to the one described on page 11 (compost Code 1), and firm it down with a firming board (see Fig 8). Large seeds should be spaced out over the surface of the compost, whilst small seeds can be sprinkled, spacing them as much as possible at the same time.

Step three Cover the large seeds with a 5–7cm (¼–½in) layer of compost. The small seeds should have a fine layer, just enough to cover the seed. Very fine seeds should not be covered. When compost *is* applied, it should be done by passing it through a sieve.

Step four Water the seeds, using a watering-can with a fine rose. First start the

15

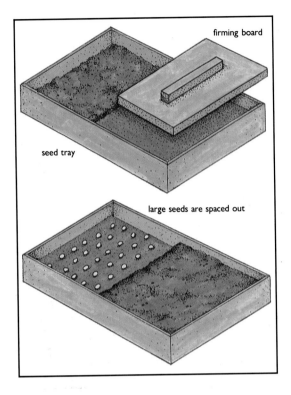

Fig 8 Do not cover very fine seeds with compost.

water flow away from the tray, then move it backwards and forwards across the compost area, moving the can away from the tray before it runs out of water. By doing this you will not puddle or form holes in the compost, which in turn would bury or wash away the seeds.

Step five When the seeds have developed their first seed leaves and are large enough to handle, pot them (prick them out) into small pots, using a compost Code 4 for young seedlings, as shown in the soil section of the book. Care should be taken not to damage the stem when pricking out.

Damping Off

One of the most troublesome and probably the most common problem for the beginner when growing bonsai from seed, is a soil-borne fungus (*pythium and rhizoctonia solani*) disease termed damping off. The stem is damaged at the soil level or just above, roots may rot and you are left with a black stump covered in a grey mould (*Botrytis cinerea*). The chemical control offered on the shelves of garden centres is not very effective. Copper fungicide, backed up by good standards of hygiene such as clean seed trays and partially sterilised compost is the best possible prevention against the disease. As far as possible, try to follow these instructions:

1 Always wash seed trays with a horticultural disinfectant before using them.
2 Never use the same seed compost to sow a second batch of seeds.
3 Make sure that the tray never becomes water-logged and try to control the level of humidity, keeping it to a minimum.
4 Spray with a copper fungicide.

After-Care

Protect from strong winds, heavy rain and frost. Look out for pests that will eat the young foliage.

OUTDOOR SEEDS

Seeds of the hardy outdoor bonsai are sown September to October, or March to April. The procedure for outside sowing is basically the same as that of indoor, except a little more sharp sand is used to help the drainage. Use compost Code 1. Stand the seed tray away from over-hanging trees or a gutter that may drip and place them on a table or bench where dogs can't abuse the seed tray, or cats use it as a litter tray. Nets can be erected if birds become a problem.

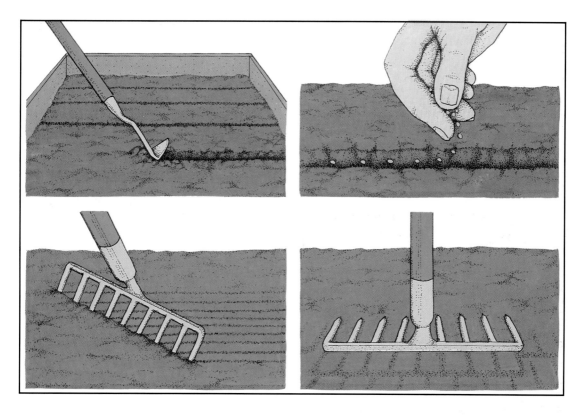

Fig 9   Basic gardening traditions are used when sowing seeds out of doors

Soil Sown Seeds

There is a large variety of seed which can be sown direct into a prepared site, made with wooden sides as shown in Fig 9. Seeds such as oak and horse chestnut should germinate in the spring without too many problems after being sown in the autumn.

Autumn Sowing

Step one   Prepare the bed for sowing your seeds by digging the soil and removing any weeds, especially the perennial type. Firm the soil by walking over the surface and pushing down with your heels, taking out any hollows. Be careful not to pack the soil down too hard otherwise you will impede the drainage (or pan the soil).

Step two   Make a drill about the same depth as the seed. Using the corner of a draw hoe, carefully space the seed, sowing along the length of the drill. Cover the seed with the soil from the drill and firm it with the back of a rake.

Spring Sowing

Step one   The bed for spring planting should be forked over in the late autumn ready for sowing the following spring. Roughly dig the soil, leaving it in large lumps for the frost to break down over the winter period.

Step two   Lightly fork over the bed, breaking down any large lumps left from the winter frost treatment. Walk over the bed pushing down with your heels, then with a rake work

17

the soil until you form a fine tilth. (Tilth is a crumb formation which is very beneficial to seeds and trees growing in it. The particles formed in a tilth have small pores which retain moisture, but at the same time help to form a passageway for the movement of water and air.)

Step three Sowing the seed in seed drills is the same as for autumn.

Before attempting to sow your seeds, read through the following list telling you where and when to sow them.

Seed Sowing Guide

Tree Seed	March/April	September/October	Outside	Under Cover
Acer (Maple)	●			●
or		●	●	
Aesculus (Horse Chestnut)		●	●	
Arbutus (Strawberry Tree)	●			●
Berberis	●			●
Betula (Silver Birch)	●		●	
Buxus (Box)		●		●
Carpinus (Hornbeam)	●		●	
Castanea (Sweet Chestnut)		●		●
Catalpa (Indian Bean)	●		●	
Cedrus (Cedar)	●			●
Cercis (Judas Tree)	●			●
Chaenomeles	●		●	
Cotoneaster	●		●	
Crataegus (Hawthorn)	●		●	
Cryptomeria	●		●	
Cupressus	●		●	
Fagus (Beech)	●		●	
Fraxinus (Ash)	●	●	●	
Ginkgo (Maidenhair Tree)	●			●
Ilex (Holly)	●		●	
Juglans (Walnut)	●		●	
Juniperus (Juniper)	●		●	
Laburnum (Golden Rain)	●		●	
Larix (Larch)	●		●	
Liquidambar (Sweet Gum)	●		●	

Tree Seed	March/April	September/October	Outside	Under Cover
Liriodendron (Tulip Tree)	●		●	
Malus (Crab Apple)	●		●	
Nothofagus (Southern Beech)	●		●	
Podocarpus	●			●
Prunus (Cherry)	●			●
Pseudotsuga (Japanese Douglas Fir)	●		●	
Pyracantha (Fire Thorn)	●			●
Quercus (Oak)		●	●	
Rhododendron and Azalea	●			●
Rhus (Sumach)	●			●
Robinia (False Acacia)	●			●
Sequoia (Redwood)	●		●	
Sequoiadendron (Wellingtonia)	●		●	
Sorbus (Mountain Ash)	●		●	
Stewartia	●			●
Syringa (Lilac)	●			●
Taxodium (Swamp Cypress)	●			●
Taxus (Yew)	●		●	
Tilia (Lime)		●	●	
Ulmus (Elm)		●	●	
Wisteria	●			●
Zelkova (Grey Bark Elm)	●		●	

PROPAGATION OF CUTTINGS

The propagation of cuttings as described below is directed toward the hardy bonsai. Indoor bonsai material, or less hardy as we will term them from now on, can be taken in the same way, but only as for the softwood cuttings, with bottom heat, or as semi-ripe cuttings taken in the summer. The difference comes at the end of the summer when the hardy bonsai will tolerate low temperatures, but the less hardy bonsai will need 15–21°C (60–70°F) and a totally frost-free position.

There are three types of cuttings: softwood, semi-ripe and hardwood. Softwood are cuttings taken from the current season's wood, and can be taken from April to June and also in January if heat is used. Semi-ripe are also taken from the current season's wood. The base of this cutting should be woody, and taken from July to October. Hardwood is current season's wood that has ripened. Most hardwood cuttings will root without heat or cover from November to December.

Collect strong, healthy side-shoots; the best time to do this is first thing in the morning. Place all material collected in plastic bags to stop it from drying out. Always pick non-flowering material that is free from pests and diseases. The cutting compost for all pots and trays is Code 2.

Softwood

Preparation

Cut just below a node (see Fig 10(a)). The length should be between 5cm (2in) and 7.5cm (3in). The leaves from the lower part of the cutting should be removed (Fig 10(b)). Dip the base of the cutting into a rooting hormone and push it gently into your cutting compost. Place the cuttings under mist or on to a warm bench. (see page 24).

After-Care

If the tips of the cutting are starting to shoot and a white root system can be seen, this is a

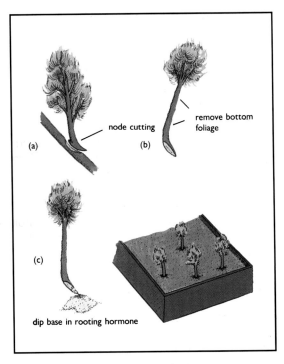

Fig 11   Most semi-ripe cuttings will root without bottom heat.

sign that the cuttings have taken. Remove the cuttings from the tray and pot them individually into small pots containing one of the soils described in chapter 1.

Semi-Ripe

Preparation

The collection preparation for semi-ripe cuttings is very similar to the softwood cutting but they should be slightly longer at 5–10cm (4–6in). This is the type of cutting to do if you are unable to provide artificial heat, as shown in Fig 11.

After-Care

Check for new growth and a white root system. If the cuttings have rooted, pot as for the softwood cutting. If grown in a cold frame,

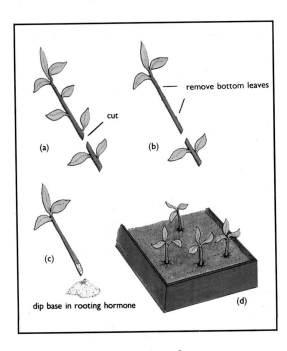

Fig 10   Never use flowering shoots for cuttings.

give them ventilation on warm days, and start to harden them off ready for the winter. Leave the cuttings to over-winter in the frame until the following spring.

Training Softwood and Semi-Ripe Cuttings

Once the cuttings have taken root, move them into individual pots and place them back into the same temperature for the next week or two. After this period, move them closer to the door if grown in a glasshouse, leave the top slightly open if grown in a cold frame, or pull back the plastic if grown in a low tunnel. If using a small propagator, lower the temperature and allow more air to enter. This will give the seedlings a chance to acclimatise to the weather conditions outside the growing area. Pinch out the growing tips during the first year, but do not attempt to prune the root system at this stage. Check the watering requirement every day, feed with a balanced fertiliser every three weeks, and spray for pests and diseases.

Hardwood

Preparation

Collect hardwood cuttings during November and choose well ripened cuttings of the current season's wood. The cuttings should be between 15–25cm (6–9in) long. The top and the bottom should look like that in Fig 12.

Training

Hardwood cuttings will not need the hardening-off period of softwood and semi-ripe, but they should still be protected from frost and strong winds. They should be left in the soil after planting in November (year one) to the following March of year three. During this time the growing tips should be pinched back hard to keep the growth under control.

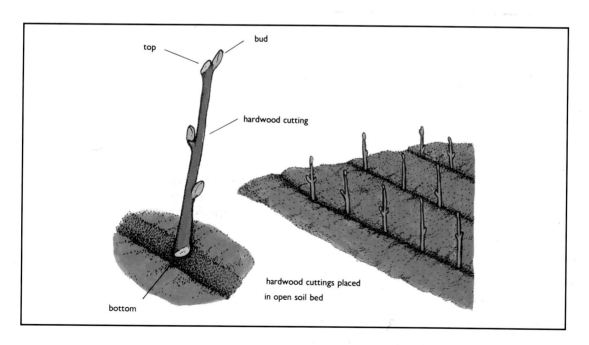

Fig 12 Hardwood cuttings can be the cheapest form of propagation.

Water before the soil dries out, and feed every three weeks with a balanced fertiliser. Spray for pests and diseases.

CUTTINGS IN SMALL AMOUNTS

There are people who will only grow five or six cuttings and don't have the time or the space to take cuttings on a large scale. There are two options open to them: the use of basic equipment such as a pot, wire and polythene without any form of heat; or the purchase of an electric propagator.

Basic Equipment

Below is a step-by-step guide to growing small amounts of *semi-ripe* cuttings with very basic equipment and without bottom heat.

Step one   Purchase a normal plastic plant pot from your local garden centre and cover with a propagating cover.

Step two   Fill the pot with cutting mix Code 2. Choose your semi-ripe cutting material and prepare the cuttings as described previously.

Step three   When the cutting is ready, make holes around the outside of the pot with a dibber or chopstick and transplant your cuttings.

Step four   Water the compost and allow the excess water to drain away, then secure the plastic top, or a plastic bag with a wire frame used as an alternative to the plastic top (see Fig 17). After-care is the same as described earlier for semi-ripe cuttings.

Electric Propagator Method

For those people who would like more than the odd cutting or two but still want to

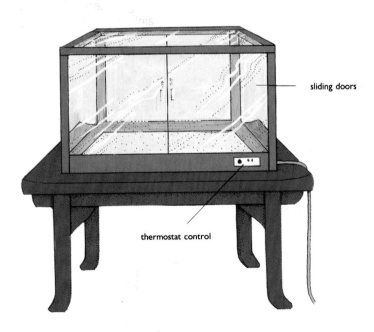

sliding doors

thermostat control

Fig 13   A simple electric propagator will give you more control when taking cuttings.

propagate only on a small scale, a small electric propagator from your local garden centre is the ideal solution. With such a tool you could grow softwood and semi-ripe cuttings without too many problems, but choose carefully when buying the propagator and make sure it has a thermostat control on it. In the garden centre you will also find plastic tops which are made to fit pots and trays; these are fine from May to August, but they haven't the same degree of control as that of an electric propagator. Fig 13 shows one type of propagating case available; note that this one has sliding doors for ventilation and access.

If you choose a propagator with a thermostat it will give you more control over the temperature. Because it is electric you will need to be close to a power point, which may be a problem because you will also need to choose an area with plenty of light. You can overcome the problem of the power point by using an extension lead, but remember, *never* allow the extension lead to come into contact with water and *always* extend the cable to its full length, otherwise the cable will overheat and may cause a fire.

Step one Turn on the propagator and allow the temperature to reach the desired level. This is governed by the type of cutting and the time of year.

Step two Take your cuttings in the same way as described for softwood or semi-ripe cuttings then place the tray or pot into the propagator. With the advantage of bottom heat the cutting should root in four weeks.

CUTTINGS ON A LARGER SCALE

For those who have the space and time it is far better to plan and build your own bonsai propagation area, which could also be useful for storage and soil planting.

There are five ways in which I produce my cutting material. The first is a mist unit used mainly for softwood cuttings. The second is

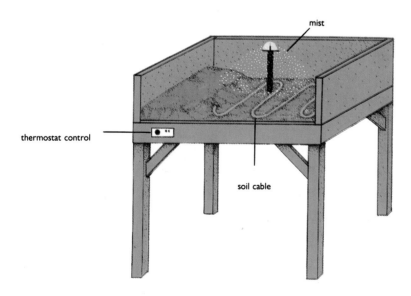

Fig 14   A basic mist unit is ideal for growing cuttings.

the warm bench, also used for softwood cuttings, but for those which do not like conditions too wet. The third is a cold frame, which is where I grow most of my semi-ripe cuttings. The fourth is a low polythene tunnel where I grow semi-ripe cuttings but temperature control can be a problem during a hot summer. The fifth is to grow them in the open ground.

Mist Unit

The mist unit is a form of bench with electric warming cables running through a sand and gravel base. These cables are controlled by a thermostat and the temperature is kept around 20°C (70°F). A circuit-breaker called an 'electric leaf' is fitted, which turns the mist jets on and off, keeping the area humid. Fig 14 shows a large mist unit, but for the person who will only take fifty to one hundred cuttings, there are small mist units available.

Warm Bench

As you can see in Fig 15, a warm bench is a bench with sides, a very fine mesh (less than 4mm) covering the bottom to allow drainage. This is covered with 6mm gravel, on top of which a thin layer of mixed sand and gravel is spread. An electric warming cable is then placed on top in several 'U' shapes, one end connected to a thermostat which controls the temperature. More sand is added on top of the cables. When plugged in, the cables heat up the sand which gives bottom heat to the pots containing the cuttings.

Cold Frame

There are many cold frames on the market and many, it is sad to say, are of poor quality. The old brick or wood cold frame is hard to come by unless you are a D.I.Y. person. The type of cold frame we are looking for should

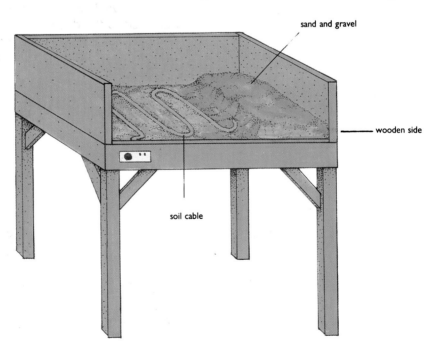

sand and gravel

wooden side

soil cable

Fig 15   The warm bench is the same as the mist unit but without the misting effect.

be well made, of brick or wood and lined with polythene. The lid must fit securely, but be easily removed to allow ventilation and hardening off. The bottom of the cold frame will need good drainage, which can be obtained by digging a hole the same shape as the cold frame and filling it with hardcore and gravel. An electric warming cable could be fitted in

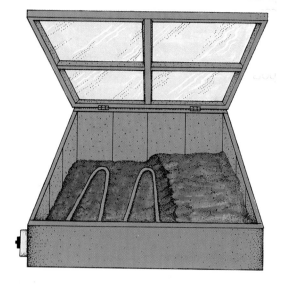

Fig 16   The everyday cold frame can be adapted to bonsai growing by adding a soil cable to the bottom of it.

the bottom, making a cold frame *and* a warm bench, which could also be used to overwinter your bonsai during periods of very low temperature (see Fig 16).

Low Polythene Tunnels

The tunnel could be made of polythene or plastic. In the past, most low tunnels were made of glass; you can still use this if you wish, but you will find it more expensive to use than the other two. One problem with the plastic is that it will not roll back during warm spells in the summer. I therefore use polythene to cover the tunnel, as shown in Fig 17.

Open Ground

The area chosen for rooting cuttings in the open should be sheltered, have a south-facing aspect, be out of heavy shade and strong winds, and have good drainage. The area should have been marked out and the soil removed to the depth of a spade. The trench is then filled, first with hardcore and then with gravel. A mound of compost comprising moss peat, sand and a compost containing loam is placed on top as shown in Fig 18. This area could also be used for growing bonsai in the soil.

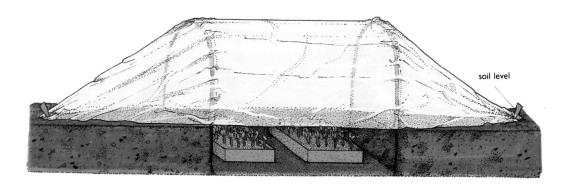

soil level

Fig 17   A cheap and easy way of creating a plastic tunnel.

25

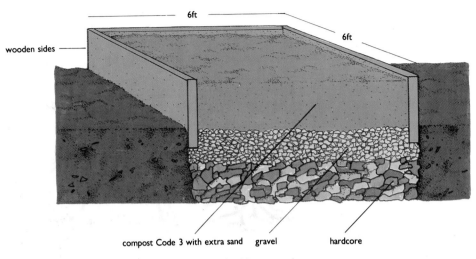

Fig 18 By building sides made of wood or brick, and adding a good drainage system, you will make the ideal outdoor growing area.

wooden sides

6ft

6ft

compost Code 3 with extra sand   gravel   hardcore

Cutting List

Japanese Maple During April, *Acer palmatum* cuttings should be placed in a tray with a compost mixture of two parts moss peat to one part sand. The tray is then placed either under mist, on a warm bench or small propagator, or under a low plastic tunnel in June as a semi-ripe cutting. Personally I prefer to use a warm bench which stops the Maple cuttings from becoming too wet. The cuttings should take root after four weeks.

Berberis These can be taken as hardwood cuttings. Some smaller varieties, such as those ending with the name 'nana', can be propagated by division of the root ball during the autumn.

Buxus Commonly known as 'box', this is a very slow-growing shrub and can make very interesting bonsai. Hardwood cuttings are taken in November, smaller varieties can be propagated by division in April.

Chaenomeles Known by two other names, Japanese quince and cydonia, chaenomeles

Fig 19 Small cotoneaster, 7 years old.

26

Fig 20   Chinese juniper, 35 years old.

will make a nice flowering bonsai. The flowers are very colourful, but tend to be too large for the tree. Softwood cuttings are taken in June and put in a cold frame, low plastic tunnel or unheated propagator.

Cornus The cornus is also called 'dogwood'; the one I use for bonsai is called *Cornus* and produces yellow flowers in February. Hardwood cuttings are taken in November. Cuttings can also be taken in October, but would need to be placed in a cold frame or small, unheated propagator.

Cotoneaster *Cotoneaster horizontalis* is the most popular form in bonsai. With its weeping, herring-bone branch work, it will make a good, informal bonsai. To add to this you have white flowers in the spring and red berries in the winter. Cuttings are taken in June and placed under mist, low plastic tunnel or in an unheated propagator.

Jasminum *Jasminum nudiflorum* is the best form to use for bonsai. It has yellow flowers during the early part of the winter, and displays well if grown over rock. Hardwood cuttings are taken in November.

Juniperus Two forms of juniper are used, *Juniperus chinensis* and *Juniperus rigida*. Cuttings for *J. chinensis* are taken in April and put under mist. Cuttings for *J. rigida* are also taken in April, but placed in a cold frame or small propagator.

LAYERING

Layering is a good alternative to cuttings when you are trying to propagate bonsai material which tends to be slow or difficult to root. There are several ways of layering; simple layering, continuous layering, which is also termed 'French layering', and serpentine

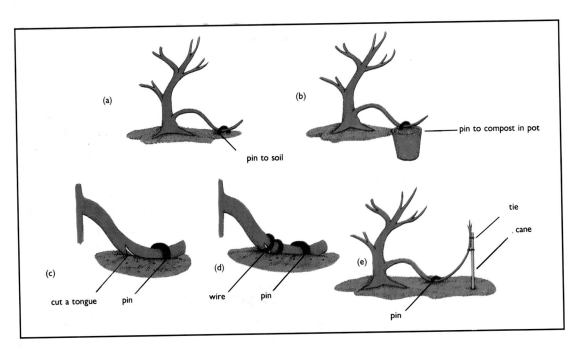

Fig 21 *Layering is a good way of propagating trees which are difficult to propagate from normal cuttings.*

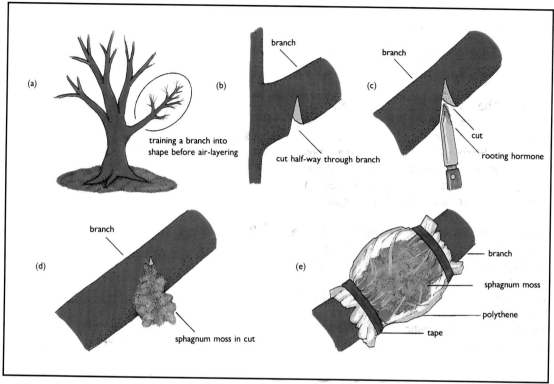

Fig 22   Air layering is a good way to produce a mature tree in a short space of time, and is also used to shorten leggy trunks.

layering. The best time to perform layering is between April and July.

Simple Layering

Take hold of a branch of the plant to be propagated and pin it to the surface of the soil, or the soil level if grown in a pot, as shown in Figs 21(a) and (b). Once the branch has been pinned you will need to interrupt the sap flow of the plant. This can be accomplished in two ways: either cut a tongue below the bend as shown in Fig 21(c); or place a piece of wire, such as the type used for bonsai wiring, around the bark at the bend as shown in Fig 21(d). In some layering techniques, such as that used for rhododendrons, a stake is placed at one end as shown in Fig 21(e).

Continuous Layering

Almost the same as simple layering, continuous layering uses more pins to hold the branch at a horizontal plane, to force the root system along the complete length of the underside of the branch. This encourages the buds to grow into upright shoots. When both roots and shoots are showing healthy growth, the rooted section can be cut away from the mother tree and will be the beginnings of a bonsai raft as shown in Fig 69.

Serpentine Layering

This is a good way of producing wisteria, and is very similar to continuous layering. Instead of pinning the branch to the soil, however, chosen sections are buried, leaving a bud

29

showing which in turn grows into a stem whilst the bottom develops a root system. When the roots and shoots have developed strong, healthy growth, each section is cut away.

AIR-LAYERING

Many bonsai are started by this process, mainly because it is possible to air-layer old wood as well as young. The young wood will root within twelve months, but older wood may take longer. The advantages with this form of propagation are that trees with a thick trunk can be produced in a short space of time, and trees which would normally be too tall, or as we term it too 'leggy', can still be used.

The first thing you need to do is to pick a suitable branch or area just above the 'leggy' section which possesses the thickness of trunk you have in mind and a well-spaced network of branches. The part of the tree chosen for air-layering can be encouraged to grow in the desired shape by pruning one or two years before propagation takes place as shown in Fig 22(a).

Having chosen or prepared a suitable branch, make a cut half-way through the branch or at the base of your future trunk as shown in Fig 22(b). This is called 'wounding'. Next, dust the blade of your knife with a rooting hormone, the type used for semi-ripe and hardwood cuttings, and run the blade through the cut you have just made, wiping the hormone powder from the blade into the cut (Fig 22(c)).

The cut should then be kept open by packing moist sphagnum moss into it (Fig 22(d)). More moist sphagnum moss is added outside the cut, and the treated section of the branch is wrapped in clear polythene and sealed at both ends with tape (Fig 22(e)). When the polythene is filled with a white root growth, the air-layer can be removed from the mother tree.

GRAFTING

Grafting, to the bonsai beginner, is probably the hardest form of propagation and it can take several years to acquire such skills. When finally mastered, however, it will enable you to propagate trees such as crab apple, cherry and plum. It can also give satisfying results, when grafting two colours on to one branch.

Grafting is the act of forming a 'union' between two separate parts of a tree, the lower or root area called a 'rootstock' and a top piece called a 'scion'.

Rootstock

Before learning how to graft, you should first understand more about the rootstock. The compatible rootstock for most of the trees used for bonsai are listed below.

Tree	Recommended Rootstock
Maple (Acer, most types)	Acer palmatum
Maple (English Sycamore)	Acer pseudoplatanus
Maple (Norway)	Acer platanoides
Hawthorn (Crataegus)	Crataegus monogyna
Beech (Fagus)	Fagus sylvatica
Crab Apple (Malus)	Malus sylvestris
Cherries (Prunus)	Prunus avium
Mountain Ash (Sorbus)	Sorbus aucuparia
Cedar (Cedrus)	Cedrus deodara
Juniper (Juniperus)	Juniperus virginiana
Larch (Larix)	Larix decidua
Rhododendron	Rhododendron ponticum
Spruce (Picea)	Picea abies
Spruce (Picea)	Picea pungens (Blue)
Pines (Pinus)	Pinus thunbergii
Yew (Taxus)	Taxus baccata

Materials

Raffia is a tough string-like material used to hold the two surfaces together firmly but not too tightly, as shown in Figs 25 and 26. Grafting wax is used to help keep water out of the union and also stops the area from drying out. The wax is heated, then applied with a brush.

Types of Graft

There are several ways of grafting, but I only use four to grow bonsai: whip-and-tongue, cleft graft, saddle graft and veneer graft.

Whip-and-Tongue

Dormant wood is used for this common form of grafting, which is carried out between February and March outside in a sheltered spot or in an unheated glasshouse. First cut the rootstock as shown in Fig 23. The scion should have been chosen during the previous

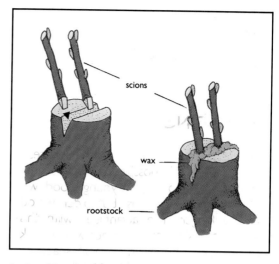

Fig 24   Cleft graft. Handy for developing a thick trunk with several top branches.

growing season. Prepare the scion as shown in Fig 23. Tie the graft with raffia and apply wax.

Cleft Graft

This is a good way to produce a bonsai with a thick trunk and a network of top branches. The rootstock used for the cleft graft is much thicker than the scion or scions. A 'V' shape cut is made at the top of the rootstock and the scion is wedged into this cut as shown in Fig 24. The graft is then wrapped with raffia and waxed.

Saddle Graft

I very seldom use this type of graft, when I do it is only to grow bonsai rhododendrons. For this type of graft, the rootstock and scion need to be of the same thickness. Saddle grafting on rhododendrons is carried out during the winter months. The root used for the rhododendron is that of *Rhododendron ponticum*, and is placed on a warm bench (as shown in the propagation section) or plunged into peat between the months of November

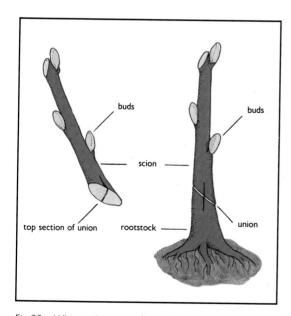

Fig 23   Whip-and-tongue graft. It is very important to link up the cambium layers.

31

and December with a bottom heat temperature of 21°C (70°F).

Step one   Cut the root stock down to about 5cm (2in) and shape as shown in Fig 25(a). The point to remember and the difference between normal grafting for shrubs and trees to be planted as part of the garden and bonsai is that we are trying to create a small, attractive bonsai and the position of and

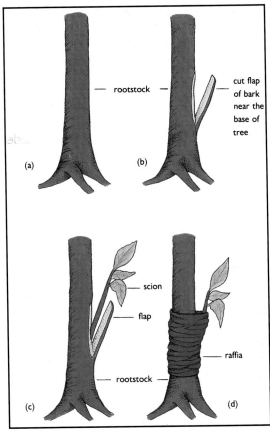

Fig 26   Veneer graft. An ideal graft for a twin trunk tree or producing a tree with two different coloured flowers.

ability to hide the graft at a later stage is a very important factor to take into consideration.

Step two   The same applies to the scion or part to be grafted on to the root stock; that is, they must match to form a non-bulky union which at a later date will form a trunk with interest. Therefore, carefully cut the scion to fit the root stock exactly with the two cambium layers making full contact. (Fig 25(b)).

Step three   The two parts should now be tightly held together by tying raffia around the union as shown in Fig 25(c).

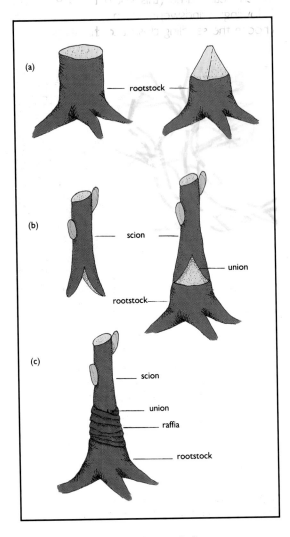

Fig 25   Saddle graft. I use this mainly for rhododendrons.

32

Step four The root stock and scion should continue to receive bottom heat until such time that the graft has taken.

Veneer Graft

Again, bottom heat is advisable with this graft. The end of the scion is shaped to match the cambium layer, then placed into the cut made low down on the rootstock as shown in Fig 26(c). The whole is then bound together with raffia.

NURSERY AND GARDEN CENTRE STOCK

There is no such thing as an instant bonsai; even the old Japanese trees collected from the wild would still need two to five years to become adjusted to the bonsai treatment. The same applies to the trees and shrubs found at your local garden centre, where they tend to stock trees which stand two to three metres high, making them totally unsuitable for bonsai.

The type of nursery you should be looking for is the one which specialises in growing trees and shrubs; here you will find cuttings and seedlings suitable for bonsai growing. If you have a friendly nursery close by, ask if they will save you some of their throw-outs. They could be throw-outs due to having twisted trunks, stunted growth or missing branches, but these could make excellent bonsai.

Height

The first thing you should look at in nursery stock is height. The seedling should be between 5–15cm (2–6in), although larger trees up to 30cm (12in) can be used. After two or three years of bonsai growing, you should feel more confident and will be able to collect much older and larger trees from the wild, but

for the time being it is far better to keep to the smaller seedling.

Shape

The second thing to look for is shape. A balanced form with plenty of character would be ideal, but this is not always possible. Therefore, picture in your mind's eye the shape and style you would like to accomplish in ten years' time (this could be one of the following: windswept, formal, informal) and choose the seedling closest to this shape.

Fig 27   A good seedling. This one is a Zelkova, 2 years old and 15cm (6in) tall.

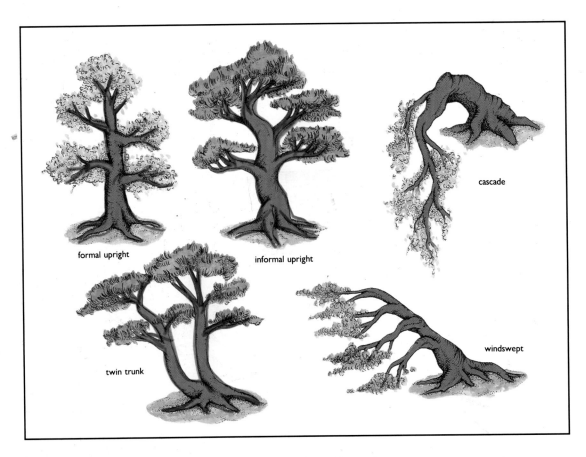

Fig 28   Basic shapes the beginner should stick to in the early stages of bonsai learning.

Roots

The third aspect to consider is the surface root system. When you first look at your seedling you are most likely to find that the base of the trunk disappears at soil level. Carefully remove the soil from the base of the trunk and see if there are any roots to expose; by exposing roots you will add to the character and give an aged appearance to the tree.

Bare-Rooted Seedlings

If you buy a seedling which has been grown in soil, such as a hardwood cutting, try as far as possible to buy a young, one to two-year-old seedling. After two years the root system will become too long and woody, and less fibrous. The other problem with soil-grown seedlings is height. A two-year-old seedling, or 'whip', can be up to one metre in height.

CHAPTER 4

Five Year Training for Hardy Bonsai

Now that you have an idea of the type of material suitable for your bonsai tree, whether grown from a seed, a cutting, or purchased at your local nursery, and you have found out which of the soils your tree will grow in, you are ready to take the first steps to growing a bonsai. For the beginner I would advise starting with a tree that is fairly easy, such as zelkova (grey bark elm), cotoneaster or hawthorn. Oak and horse chestnut, although very easy to propagate or find seedlings for, can be frustratingly difficult because of their leaf size. On the other end of the scale, trees such as pine should be left until you have gained experience and studied its growing habits.

	Root/ Germinate	Root Prune
Seed/ Softwood Cuttings	Spring year 1	Spring year 2
Semi-Ripe Cuttings	Summer year 1	Spring year 3
Hardwood Cuttings	Autumn year 1	Spring year 3

MARCH (YEAR ONE)

Root Pruning

The seedling, whether grown from seed or cutting, should be between one and two years old before starting this programme. A seed germinated (or a softwood cutting rooted) in the *spring* of year one, will start its root training the following spring (year two), but a cutting which had formed a root system by the late summer or autumn of year one would not start its root training until the spring of year three. A nursery stock seedling should have an established root system and therefore can start its root training the first March after purchase.

Fig 29 **Root Pruning.** *(a) Buds starting to swell on a maple; this is the best time to root prune.*

35

(b)   Tree and tools before root pruning.

The best time for root pruning is between March and April, and is governed by where you live in Britain. For those living in Scotland it could be late April, but for those in the south of England, early March. Therefore, as a guide keep an eye on the buds. The time to root prune is when they start to move. The first thing to do is to remove the seedling from its pot, then working from the sides down to the bottom, loosen one third of the root system as shown in Fig 29(d). Check the root system at this stage for pests, or signs of disease, then cut the roots as shown in Fig 29(e).

Re-Potting

After you have pruned the root system, the tree will need a training pot, and there is no reason why you may not use a bonsai pot if

you want to, provided it is not too shallow. The training pot can be either a half pot, or a small seed tray. Both will need holes in the bottom for the drainage. Cover the drainage hole with mesh then place your tree in the pot and gently work soil down and in between the roots with a dibber or chopstick (Fig 30(a) to (c)). Do not fill with soil to the top of the pot, so you can water without washing the soil away. Over the next two weeks do not feed or over-water the tree, and keep it out of heavy rain, strong winds and frost if kept outside.

When re-potting, I cannot over-emphasise the importance of working the compost carefully into the root area. At all costs you must avoid forming three levels; a gravel level, a root level and a top soil level. If these three levels are allowed to form, the root system remains in level two without a supply of fresh soil, which in turn hinders new root formation.

(c)   Remove the tree from its pot.

(d) (Above) Starting from the side, loosen one third of the root system, down to the bottom of the tree.

(e) (above right) Cut away one-third of the root system.

*Fig 30 (Right) **Re-Potting.** (a) Cover the pot's drainage hole with mesh.*

By mixing the two top levels together, the roots gain from fresh compost, new air and drainage passages.

Placement

Before we go any further I think it would be best to look at where you will keep the bonsai seedling during the next five years. This section relates to the whole five year growing plan and covers spring, summer and winter placement for outdoor hardy bonsai. The placement of indoor bonsai will be covered later in the book.

(b) (Above left) Place 6mm gravel at the bottom of the pot.

(c) (Left) Work the compost in between the root system with a dibber.

(d) (Above) Placing 4mm gravel on the surface of the compost will help to keep the compost moist and help to control the surface weeds.

Dangers in Spring

Frost is a major problem in the spring, unlike in autumn when the trees slip gradually into coping with the lower temperatures and autumn frost. Spring frost can seriously damage new bud and foliage; this damage results in leaves black and scorched around the edges, buds failing to burst and shoots dying back to old wood.

The result of such damage is poor growth throughout the coming growing season, and such a tree should forgo any bonsai training for the next year. The biggest danger of all comes during the last part of February, during March and in the first part of April when you will get the odd few days or weeks of bright sunshine with a rise in temperature. On days like this you convince yourself that spring has finally arrived and you either place your tree outside to be damaged by night frost or start forcing it into growth (placing the tree into a warm temperature and creating an artificial bud burst). For the beginner this can cause unexpected problems, money for heating and even the death of the tree although it is no problem for the very experienced grower who needs trees for shows. Therefore, do not force your tree and be wary of frost up to the first or second week of May. During the month of May, the spring frost should have disappeared and the tree can be placed outside away from strong winds.

Wind

Strong winds will affect bonsai by drying out the soil and foliage. The faster the wind speed over the surface area of the tree, the more the tree will draw moisture from the root system, see Fig 31. This is called 'transpiration'.

Greater care should be taken during the winter months, especially when temperatures drop below zero. When the compost becomes frozen during these periods the root cannot conduct moisture, and if the tree has dropped its foliage moisture is taken from the young wood in the last season's growth, leaving it dry, lifeless and susceptible to diseases.

The effects of wind in your garden must be taken into account when choosing a site for your bonsai. Avoid the following sites, if possible: where wind hits a solid wall or fence, causing turbulence (Fig 32(a)); a wind tunnel effect caused by a passageway through two houses (Fig 32(b)); a large, open space such as a field, which allows the wind to enter all parts of the garden (Fig 32(c)).

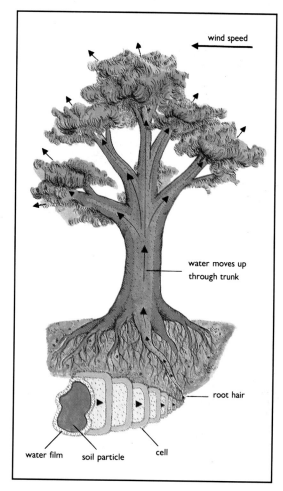

Fig 31   The faster the wind speed over the surface area, the more the tree will draw moisture from the soil particle.

Look for these potential wind problems *before* erecting a stand for your bonsai. Green mesh, similar to the type used for re-potting, fixed to the sides and top of the stand, can stop up to seventy per cent of the wind and will help to protect the tree from frost at the same time. The stand should be made of wood, with room for two or three trees, out of reach of pets and small children, and south facing if possible. The general rule for viewing a bonsai is at eye level, but you should also take into account the fact that

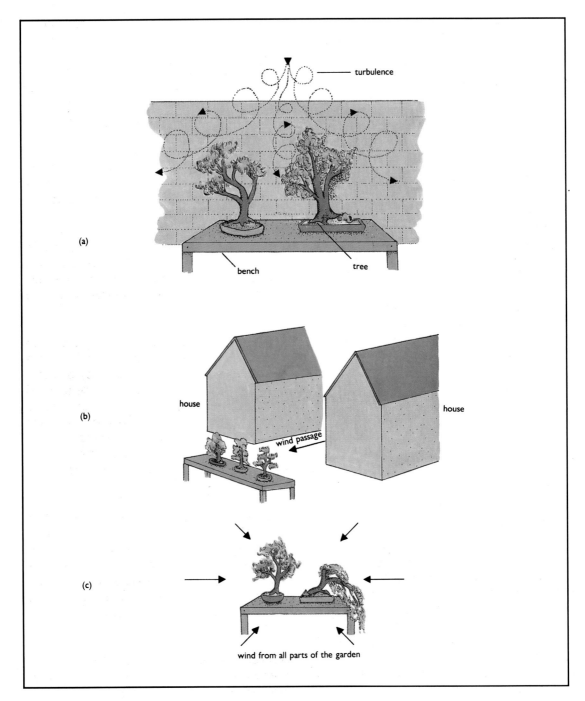

*Fig 32   Many bonsai die or are damaged through strong winds,
therefore placement is very important.*

other people will view the tree also; therefore try to find a height that will show the pot, roots, trunk and branches to their best advantage. The background behind the stand should be a light colour, such as white or blue. Never place it against a green hedge or you will loose the visual outline of the tree.

Autumn

During September and the early part of October, the temperature will slowly start to drop and the odd night frost will trigger off the autumn changes. Deciduous trees will now begin to shed their leaves. This is when a corky layer forms at the bottom of the 'petiole' or leaf stalk as it is more commonly known, interrupting the sap flow. The technical term for this corky layer is the 'abscission' layer. This corky layer blocks the flow of moisture to the leaf which then dries up and falls off. Trees such as the maple, zelkova, ginkgo and many others will take on their autumn colours of red, orange, pink and yellow. This time of year can be very confusing for beginners, especially with their first tree, as not all trees take on a distinctive autumn colour. Some become brown and crinkly, and can give the appearance of dying off, a very worrying experience.

Winter Position

Bonsai winter care has changed over the last few years, mainly because of the extremely cold winters experienced recently in Britain. Frost penetrated far deeper into the soil, affecting plants which had been growing in the garden for years. These frosts also entered cold frames and glasshouses which were previously untouched. For many years the general practice when over-wintering a bonsai has included the following:

1   Leave your bonsai standing on the bench. This is fine during mild winters with only the occasional day dropping below zero, but not for prolonged periods of cold.

2   Place a top cover or roof over the bench, with side netting that could be rolled up or down. This would give the trees protection from wind and frost, but again not from prolonged periods below zero.

3   Another way, basically the same as the last, is that instead of making a top cover the tree is placed under the bench and polythene is placed over the openings.

4   Bury the tree in the garden up to its bottom branches in clean soil. This is a good way of protecting the root system, but offers little protection from wind and frost to the top of the tree.

5   Place the bonsai into a specially-built cold frame as shown in Fig 16 (page 25). This form of protection is by far the best way of over-wintering a bonsai. It costs very little to build and offers wind, frost and snow protection. For a few extra pounds plastic bubble lining can be added and also soil warming cables if your budget will run to it. Should the weather turn mild, the top can be easily removed to control temperatures.

A glasshouse or, as most people term it, a 'greenhouse' will do the same job as a cold frame. Again, some form of heat connected to a thermostat which turns itself on when it reaches a certain temperature will keep out the frost. Such a heater can be purchased from your local garden centre, designed with a built-in frost control.

NOTE: Remember that if your bonsai is over-wintered in a cold frame or glasshouse, take care not to force the tree into growth in the spring. Lower the temperature and lift the top of the cold frame on warm, sunny days.

Although most hardy trees will tolerate very low temperatures for short periods, extra care should be given to trees in very shallow pots, trees over rocks, landscape bonsai, young seedlings and trees which have recently been root pruned.

MAY (YEAR ONE)

The tree should by now be showing signs of strong, active growth and can be placed outside in a sheltered spot, away from cats and strong winds. Start feeding with a foliar feed containing a balanced N.P.K. every three weeks. Water with rain water if possible, or boiled water that has been standing for more than twenty four hours, and remember always

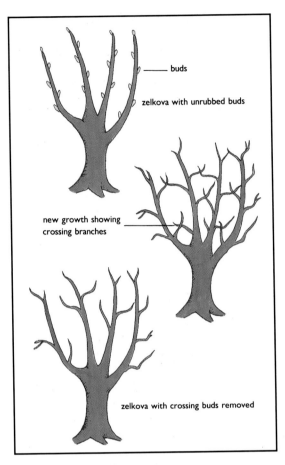

Fig 34   Rubbing out unwanted buds at the beginning will save time and overcrowding problems at a later stage.

Fig 33   Stop top growth to encourage side growth.

to water with a fine rose on the end of your watering can and before 10am or after 5pm as far as possible. Spray for pests and diseases (see pages 112 to 113).

Stop the top growth by pinching out the growing tips (see Fig 33). This will produce more branches lower down the main trunk. A strong, healthy tree is more important than its shape at this stage, although crossing branches, top and side growth will all need to be controlled. Eliminate crossing branches by rubbing out the buds as shown in Fig 34. This will save on time and die-back at a later stage.

MAY/JUNE (YEAR ONE)

Now is the time to start thinking about the shape of your tree. Shape is a very individual and personal subject; it can be based on past experience, feelings, visual and artistic skills. I will lay down basic rules to follow, but it is the decisions you make which instils your own personality and character into the tree. Therefore as a general rule make sure the tree is healthy and has a balanced form of growth, take out crossing branches to allow light and air to enter the centre of the tree, and the rest is up to you. As a guide I describe a few basic shapes step by step, but firstly, pruning techniques must be learnt.

Pruning Techniques

There are many ways of shaping your bonsai tree, but for the beginner it is far better to keep to the six basic techniques of controlling new growth, pruning to a bud, wiring, clamping the main trunk, bridging and leaf pruning. All six are what we term 'cosmetic pruning', that is to say removal of new growth and young wood. Large branch pruning, i.e. over 10mm in diameter, should only be carried out during the tree's dormant period.

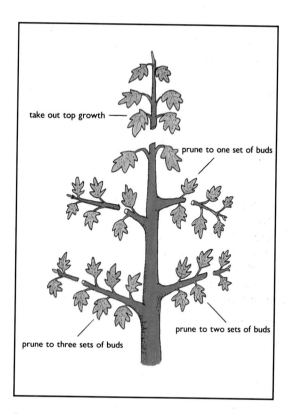

Fig 35 Stopping the top growth will force the side growth to develop. The same applies when stopping side growth when sub-lateral growth will form.

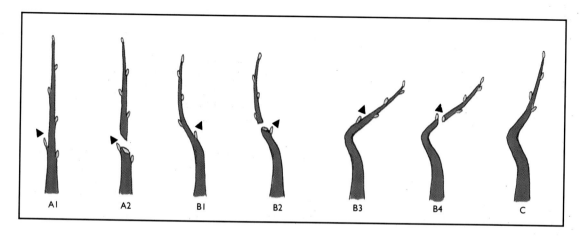

Fig 36 As far as possible, try to shape the trunk or branch from bud growth.

Controlling New Growth

Allow the new growth to develop to a desired point, then with your bonsai trimming shears (or finger and thumb if pinching junipers), cut back to the point you have chosen, as shown in Fig 35. Cosmetic pruning on pines, spruce and junipers is detailed later (see pages 60 to 62).

Pruning to a Bud

Pruning to a bud is the natural way to shape your tree. First pick a bud which is facing the direction you would like to form a branch. By cutting back to this bud you will force the new growth in that direction, as shown in Fig 36.

Pruning Cuts

When cutting back to a bud it is very important that you make a clean cut and do not leave stumps (see Fig 37(a)). The pruning cut should

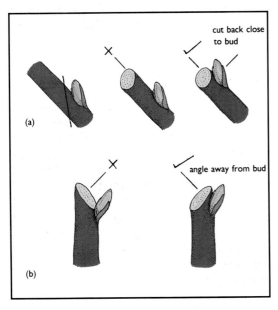

Fig 37 (a) Be sure to prune close to a bud, and (b) angle as shown to prevent a build-up of water at the base of the bud.

be angled so that water will run away from the bud or pruned area, as shown in Fig 37(b). To leave stumps or an area which will hold or direct water will cause rot, die-back and disease such as coral spot. (see page 117).

Clamping the Main Trunk

The tools used for clamping can be either specialised tools purchased from a bonsai centre or simply two or three canes as in Fig 38. Whichever of these systems is used, they should not be allowed to remain on the trunk for more than one growing season.

Wiring

Wiring should only be carried out if you are unable to shape the bonsai by pruning, and the beginner should not fall into the trap of thinking that all bonsai should be wired because they have seen pictures of wired bonsai. In fact, bonsai wire can be very damaging if used by the beginner who has not practised on an old piece of wood first. The wire should not be bound too tightly but at the same time it should be secure enough to hold the branch or trunk in the position that it has been set. At one time the only wire used for bonsai training would have been copper, but it is now made of aluminium which can be purchased in several different gauges ranging from 1.0mm to 6.0mm. The two most important rules to remember when wiring is never wire new, sappy, growth (wait until it becomes woody), and never leave the wire on for more than one growing season. Very serious damage to the bark and permanent scarring will result if it is not removed. To give added protection to those bonsai which have soft barks, cover the wire with raffia as shown in Fig 39(a).

Some imported trees have tell-tale signs of over-wiring, and some still contain pieces of wire embedded in their bark. If you should purchase such a bonsai, remove the wire as soon as possible.

Many bonsai growers, and not always the

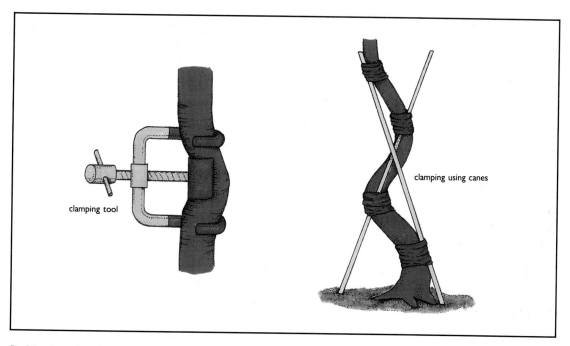

clamping tool

clamping using canes

Fig 38   A modern clamp can be used, or you can do it the old way with canes.

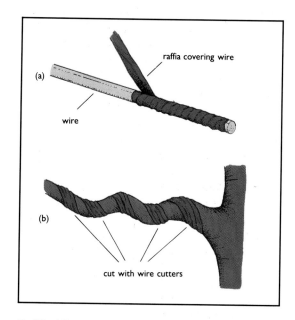

(a)

raffia covering wire

wire

(b)

cut with wire cutters

Fig 39   Wiring. (a) Raffia will help to protect the bark from damage. (b) Never try to remove the wire by unwinding. Using wire cutters, cut at the points shown.

beginner, damage branches when removing wire. Therefore, if the wire is cut at the points shown in Fig 39(b), it will fall off without damaging the branch.

Wiring the Main Trunk

Step one Bonsai seedlings between the age of one to three years old lend themselves quite readily to being shaped with wire, but for older bonsai it may be advisable to use a clamp. However, for those bonsai which have supple trunks and where the bark has started to become woody, start by first cutting a length of wire slightly longer than the trunk. Push the wire into the soil; the anchoring of the wire plays a very important part in keeping the wire firm, therefore helping to hold the position you are about to create.

Step two Working upwards, wrap the wire around the trunk. The gauge of wire used depends on the thickness of the trunk.

45

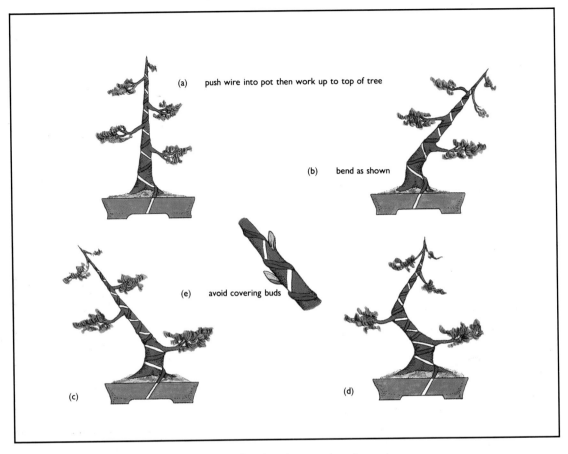

(a) push wire into pot then work up to top of tree

(b) bend as shown

(e) avoid covering buds

(c)

(d)

Fig 40   Shaping the main trunk with wire. Never allow the wire to cut into the trunk.

Step three   Hold the base of the tree firmly with one hand, then with the other hand carefully bend and twist the trunk until you reach the desired shape as seen in Fig 40(b) to (d). Avoid covering buds as far as possible by positioning wire between the bud system as shown in Fig 40(e).

Wiring a Branch

Step one   The beginner will find it easier to wire two branches at the same time rather than single branches, using the centre or main trunk as an anchoring point. First choose two branches close to each other as shown in Fig 41.

Step two   Cut a piece of wire long enough to wire both branches, then start from the middle of the wire and wire branch (a), then do the same to branch (b). The most important thing to remember when wiring double or single branches is to anchor the middle of the wire first. (See chapter 6 for periods and length of time wire should remain on individual bonsai.) Remember, this is the basic technique. As you grow in experience, you will slightly change your wiring habits. Therefore, as a general rule place the wire on previous seasons's wood (remember, do not wire young, sappy growth) at the beginning of a growing season, just before bud burst.

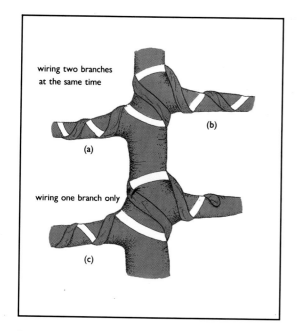

Fig 41   A good anchoring point is very important.

Bridging

I use this technique to space the branches. The bridge stops branches from rubbing and allows light and air into the centre of the tree. The bridge is made out of wood and shaped as shown in Fig 42. On the smaller branches, ice lolly sticks, cut and shaped, make ideal bridges.

Leaf Pruning

If a tree is not leaf pruned the leaves will begin to look out of keeping with the rest of the tree because they will become too large. Therefore, between the end of June and the first two weeks of July you should leaf prune your tree. The tree must be in good health, giving out strong growth, and be free from pest. Feed the tree on a balanced fertiliser three weeks before leaf pruning as this will help bud formation which in turn produces the new leaves. With trees such as oak and horse chestnut, which have very large leaves, leaf

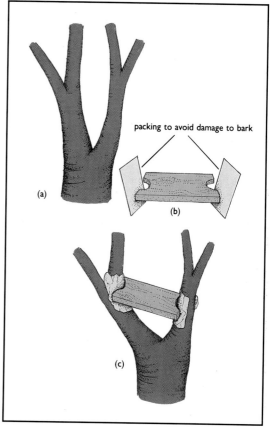

Fig 42   When bridging, take care not to split the branch by using too much force.

pruning will need to be carried out on a regular basis, but even these trees will need a rest period for some years. There are two schools of thought on the removal of leaves; one believes in the removal of the large leaves only and the second believes in pruning every leaf from the tree. I would recommend you to remove large leaves only until such time as you feel confident enough to remove all the leaves. Remove the leaf and part of the leaf stalk as shown in Fig 43.

Shapes

The normal, upright, single tree shape seen in parks and woodlands is the formal upright.

47

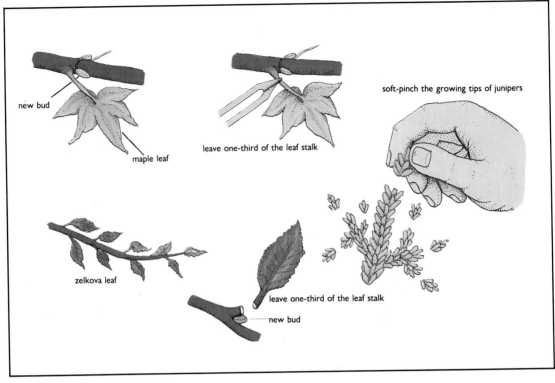

soft-pinch the growing tips of junipers

new bud

maple leaf

leave one-third of the leaf stalk

zelkova leaf

leave one-third of the leaf stalk

new bud

Fig 43   Leaf pruning. Never use tools to remove the end of junipers.

The trunk should be thick and straight with branches evenly spaced as shown in Fig 44. Twin trunks are also seen in parks and woodlands. Semi-cascades are found growing on rock faces and hillsides, and a slanting trunk is often seen growing on windy, open spaces.

FORMAL UPRIGHT

Year One

March

Step one   From the above shapes, the beginner should use the basic formal upright as a start, leading on to the other shapes at a later stage. Having said that, you will also be governed by the shape of the seedling you start with. Therefore, if the seedling is part

way to forming a cascade then continue to follow the shape already provided by nature, but if not follow the guidelines set out below by using a young seedling grown from seed or cuttings, or one that has been purchased. Choose a seedling with a straight trunk and five buds or growing points alternately spaced. Remove all other buds and growths (see Fig 45(a)). No wiring is required at this stage.

Step two   Root prune and re-pot into a training pot, as described on page 35. Allow the top growth to reach the desired height and then stop it by pinching out the growing tip (back to a bud system) as shown in Fig 45(b).

Step three   Allow the side (lateral) growth to grow until it reaches the desired point and

48

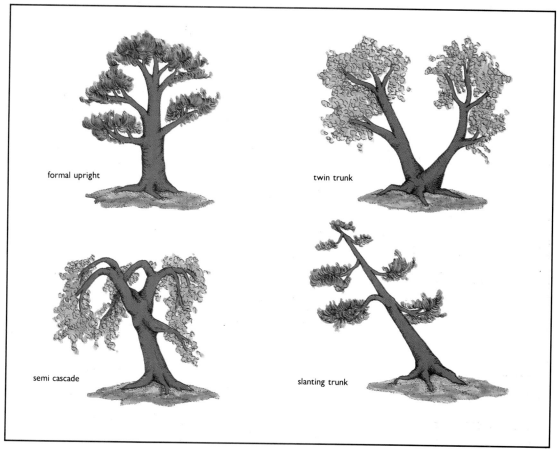

Fig 44   *The beginner should try the basic shapes before moving to more advanced styles.*

then stop it by pinching out the growing tips as seen in Fig 45(c).

Step four   When the side growing tips have been stopped, sub-lateral growth will form as in Fig 45(d). Continue to shape the tree as outlined above until you have a bold, upright, formal-looking tree.

June

Toward the end of June, change the feed from a foliar feed to a soil drench (one that is watered into the soil). Use N.P.K. of 10:14:18; this will lower the level of nitrogen and help to slow down the rate of foliage growth. Also, with a soil drench you will not run the risk of sun scorch which can occur if the feed is sprayed on to the leaves and remains on them during a hot, sunny day.

July

You may need to water twice a day, once in the morning and again in the evening. Pinch back new growth, and check underneath leaves, the ends of new growth, branches and trunk for pest. Keep up the spraying programme, but remember to avoid spraying on hot or windy days.

49

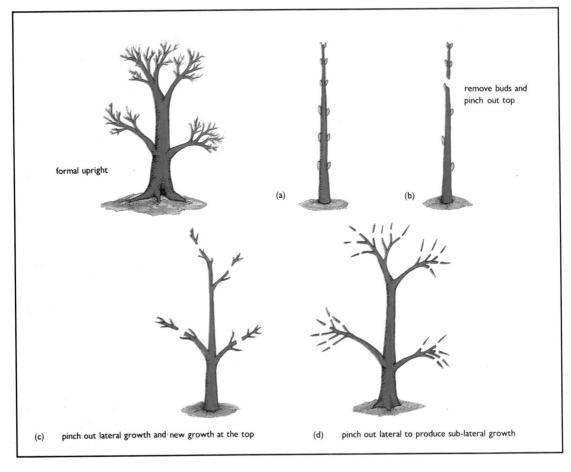

formal upright

(a)

(b) remove buds and pinch out top

(c)   pinch out lateral growth and new growth at the top

(d)   pinch out lateral to produce sub-lateral growth

Fig 45   The formal upright. The main aim is to push the strength back into the tree to produce lateral and sub-lateral side growth.

August

The growth rate should start slowing down this month. Carry on watering and spraying for pest, and towards the end of the month change the feed to a tomato feed. This is high in potash and will help to ripen and strengthen the wood for the coming winter. For those who felt the need to wire their tree, now is the time to ensure that the wire is not damaging the bark in any way.

September

With autumn and winter just around the corner, now is the time to start thinking of winter placement in cold frames and glass-houses. At one time, the general rule would have been to place your bonsai under the bench which it had been standing on all summer, but with the winters becoming more severe it would be far better to place your bonsai in one of the aforementioned positions. The rainfall for this month could now become a problem. Long periods of heavy rain will pan the soil and hinder the drainage. Therefore, shelter your tree during wet, prolonged periods. Alternatively, tilt the pot by placing a small stone or piece of wood under one end to drain away excess water.

October

Give your tree its last feed (tomato feed) during the first week of October. The autumn colours should be advancing fairly rapidly and eventually the tree, if it is the deciduous type, will move into its dormant state. Frost and strong cold winds will be your worst enemy from now on; therefore, if you have not already done so, move your tree to its winter position by the end of this month. Cut down on watering but do not allow the soil to dry out. Remove all debris such as leaves and weeds from the soil surface area of the pot. A point to make on hygiene is that a clean and tidy area, free from leaves, prunings, and old soil not only looks more attractive but will also stop troublesome pests and diseases from over-wintering in your growing area.

November to February

Now is the time, during these dormant months, to remove any branches which were too large to remove during the summer. To remove such branches you will need to use the specialised bonsai tool known as a 'fork cutter'. After removing the branch, cut around the edge of the wound with a knife as shown in Fig 48. This will help the wound to callous over and also add an aged appearance to the tree.

Year Two

March

If your tree was over-wintered in a glass-house or cold frame you will probably find that the buds will start to move at about the end of

February. As soon as the buds show signs of movement, remove the tree from the pot and follow the same procedure for root pruning and re-potting as you did for March of year one. Again, be careful not to over-water during the following two weeks and do not feed. Control the temperature to stop the tree from being forced into growth, and towards the end of the month the tree can be placed outside on warm, sunny and wind-free days for a couple of hours. However, be very careful of extreme changes in temperature and of frost. At the end of the month start feeding with a balanced N.P.K. of 7:7:7, or foliage fertiliser.

The training, watering and feeding up to March of year five is basically the same as for year one. By March of year five your tree should have a thick, bulky trunk with a dense network of small, slender branches, covered in an abundance of buds.

After Five Years

From now on the pruning, watering and feeding is the same as the first five years, but root pruning can be left for longer periods of two to three years depending on the type of tree (see chapter 6).

The root system should have developed into a compact, fibrous block, consisting of sub-lateral roots with a profusion of fine root-hairs. Prune the roots in the same way as before, but this time pot your tree into a high-class bonsai pot or dish. Picking the right size pot is important, otherwise the tree looks over-potted and this will do more damage than good to the root system. The top of the tree must balance with the roots, which in turn should just fit the pot without damaging them.

DISPLAYING

Displaying the bonsai in its pot will play a very important part in the appearance of your bonsai, and learning which is the front and the back of the tree and the right position in the pot for the tree will all add to the grace and charm of the bonsai. Choosing the front of the tree is not as easy as some people may think and even those with a trained eye can get it wrong. Again it comes down to the individual's own way of looking at the subject. However, there are a few basic rules to follow:

1   The front of the tree should express all the major good points of the tree, such as a well-spaced surface root system leading up to

a solid, firm trunk with alternately spaced, balanced lateral branches. Any pruning scars should have been shaped and calloused over.

2   The back of the tree can be chosen to hide any ugly pruning scars, large cuts due to stopping a tree grown in the soil and the less attractive lumps and bumps in the trunk of the tree, but if you have chosen your seedling wisely then the back could look almost as good as the front. The advantage of having such a balanced tree is that you are able to rotate the tree every day and allow the tree's growth to remain balanced instead of becoming one-sided.

3   Trees such as the grey bark elm (zelkova) can be grown in round pots and therefore have neither back, front or sides.

Fig 45(a)   Two young myrtles displayed in a kidney-shaped pot. Note the way the pot is designed to add water to the effect.

CHAPTER 5

Special Techniques

Bonsai growing must eventually move away from horticultural techniques, and at this point our artistic senses begin to take over, to expose roots, create abstract forms with jined branches and to hollow out old pruning wounds. For the beginner it will take time, practice and a few specialised tools to perform these techniques, and I therefore recommend you to try them first on plant material other than your favourite bonsai.

JIN

To jin is to create a branch or trunk which looks as though it has been damaged by natural elements, such as lightning, wind or old age. There are two forms of jin: where the bark is completely removed, leaving a dead-looking, white branch; and a trunk or branch which gives the appearance of live wood with old, dead parts as shown in Fig 46. Not only is

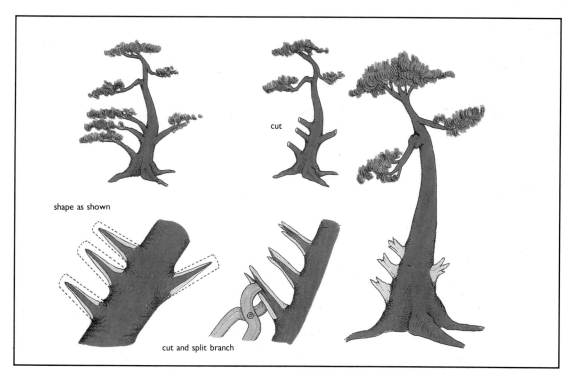

cut

shape as shown

cut and split branch

Fig 46 When the art of jining is mastered, it can look very effective, but care should be taken to stop the wood from rotting.

the bark removed to create a jin, but the wood is split and shaped to make it look natural.

Lime Sulphur

Lime sulphur used to be used to paint over the wound, turning it white or grey and preserving the wood at the same time. It has been banned from sale, mainly due to the damage it can cause to the soil or compost and therefore it will not be found at your local garden centre. I would advise the beginner to use one of the clear sealants used for fruit trees; this will not bleach the wood, but it will offer some protection.

The problem for the bonsai grower is that there is no real substitute for lime sulphur. However, one idea which has been tried is to use citrus fruit juices which will bleach the wood; but this will not protect the wood for long periods. Another idea is to allow the wounded area to remain untreated, which allows the wood to rot and take a natural course. However, care should be taken if you follow this practice, because the pith (the woody, middle part of the stem) may rot back inside the tree without being noticed, damaging parts further down the branch or trunk.

If you do decide to use lime sulphur, first cover the pot with material to avoid any contact with the compost, root system and foliage. A small paint brush or cotton bud should be used to apply the sulphur. This process should be undertaken in a well-ventilated area, preferably in the open air to avoid the extremely unpleasant fumes.

Fig 47 **Forming a callous.** *(a) A large, ugly stump left owing to bad pruning. If this is not removed it will cause damage further down the tree.*

(b)   Using a pair of fork cutters, remove the stump.

Remember to wash your hands immediately after using any chemical substances, do not drink or eat whilst using the chemical, and do not allow children to handle chemicals.

FORMING A CALLOUS

When you remove a large branch during the winter period, this may leave an ugly lump on the main trunk as shown in Fig 47(a). However, these can be worked to your advantage. By using a pair of fork cutters, as shown in Fig 47(b), you will be able to cut deeper into the trunk, forming a 'V' shape. Using a knife to remove the outer layer of bark tissue, you will expose the cambium layer which in time will callous over (Fig 47(c)).

After removing the bark, paint the centre of the wound with a clear sealant containing a fungicide, such as the type used on fruit trees. During the following year you will find that the callous hardens and takes on an aged appearance (Fig 47(d)). If you push a knife into the centre of the old pruning wound you will find that although you have covered the wound with a sealant, part of it still continues to rot. This is when you hollow out the centre, both to remove the rot, and because the hollow, with a good callous, will give the tree more character.

To hollow out the wound, take out the centre, cutting back to clean wood, and at the same time angle the bottom of the wound as shown in Fig 48, to allow water to run freely from the hollow. When you are satisfied that you have removed all the rot, paint the fresh wood with a sealant containing a fungicide.

55

(c) With a knife, remove the outer layer of tissue (the bark) to expose the cambium which will in time form a callous.

(d) This is how the callous will look at a later stage.

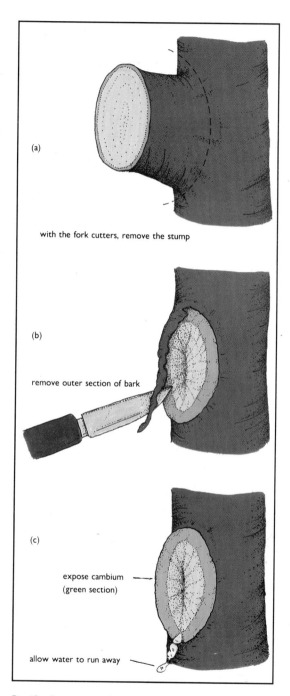

(a)

with the fork cutters, remove the stump

(b)

remove outer section of bark

(c)

expose cambium
(green section)

allow water to run away

Fig 48   Forming a callous. Allowing the water to escape will help to stop the wound from rotting.

This practice should only be carried out three or four times in a period of five years, and you should never create more than one hollow at a time.

EXPOSING ROOTS

Trees with a good surface root system tend to look much older than those with their trunks ending in a straight line (see Fig 49). As previously stated, if a good surface root system is chosen when the tree is in the seedling stage, once exposed to the elements the soft root system soon forms into a network of hard, woody surface roots, which change in thickness as the tree becomes more mature.

Fig 49   Pomegranate grown over rock, 8 years old.

SOIL GROWN BONSAI

There are two reasons why bonsai trees are grown in the soil: if the tree is in poor health and therefore needs a rest from bonsai training; or to force the trunk to grow thicker at a much faster rate. This second type of bonsai should be classed as a 'false' bonsai, created for its artistic beauty and not to be confused with a bonsai which has been truly grown with time. I use the term false bonsai with caution, because it still takes bonsai skill and several years' work to produce such a tree. Therefore, although the bonsai has been forced at the beginning to make an excellent artistic bonsai, imagine how it will look in thirty years when it also becomes an aged bonsai. The tell-tale signs which show if a

bonsai has been grown this way are termed 'chopped' or 'pollarded'. This is where the tree, whilst having its branches shaped lower down, has been allowed to grow to one or two metres high to thicken the base of the trunk, and then has been cut back hard by two-thirds or more to the shaped branches below. This leaves an ugly pruning scar which will need to be shaped and allowed to form a callous.

Year One

Between March and April, root prune your bonsai, bonsai material (such as a two-year-old seedling grown from seed), cutting or nursery stock. The seedling should contain a balanced branch system as shown in Fig 50(b).

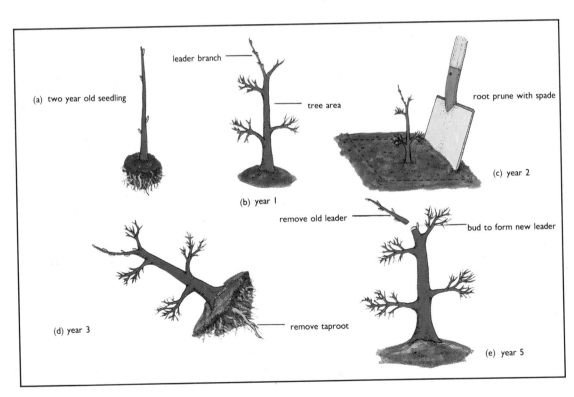

Fig 50   *The trunk of a soil grown bonsai will thicken very quickly and will give the tree the appearance of looking older than it really is. Therefore, this type of bonsai should be classed as an 'artistic' bonsai.*

Plant the bonsai in a growing area; the area used for hardwood cuttings would be suitable. Shape the trunk and branches in the same way as you would a bonsai grown in a pot, but instead of pinching out the top growth, allow it to grow in height whilst cutting back the side growth. From now on we will term the area above the trained branches a 'leader branch', and the area below, the 'tree area'. Feed and water as normal.

Year Two

Between March and April, mark a square area about 45cm (18in) from the trunk, then root prune by forcing a spade just outside of the area you mark off as shown in Fig 50(c). Continue to shape, feed and water as for the rest of year one.

Year Three

During March or April, lift the bonsai and remove the large, tap-like roots from the bottom of the root system (see Fig 50(d)). Check the roots at the same time for pests and disease, and ensure there is still a good drainage system functioning through the soil below the roots, by smelling the soil. If it has an earthy smell it is working, but if it smells like disturbed mud at the bottom of a pond, rebuild the drainage system. For the rest of the year continue to shape, feed and water as we did in years one and two. Start to train one of the buds on the leader branch, just above the tree area. This in time will be used as a replacement leader, its top growth being allowed to go on.

Year Four

Leave the roots this year and concentrate on the shape. It may be helpful at this stage to lay flat on the ground and get an eye level, or 'worm's eye level', view of the tree; at the same time block off the top with your hand and try to picture the completed bonsai in a dish. You may feel foolish doing this, but you will find a big difference in the shape looking at the tree from this angle as opposed to looking down on it. Continue to shape, feed and water as before.

Year Five

During the early part of March, take off the leader branch just above the bud you started to train in year four. Remove the bark tissue to expose the cambium, which in time will form a callous, and paint the wound with a sealant containing a fungicide. Allow this to grow on and form a new leader branch as shown in Fig 50(e). Root prune by marking an area and forcing your spade into the soil as you did in previous years.

Year Six

By now the bottom of the tree should have a trunk two or three times the size of a pot grown tree which has been growing for the same amount of time. It is now up to you to decide whether to remove it from the soil into a training pot or leave it for another two to three years in the soil. If you decide to leave the tree in the soil carry on the same procedure as before, but if you remove the tree cut the leader branch completely and follow the procedure to form a callous. At a later stage you can follow the hollowing technique to hide the scar.

When the tree is removed, you will need a training pot or tray. Whichever type you choose, make sure it has a good drainage system. After removing the tree from the soil (during March), root prune one third of its root system. Re-pot as you would for pot grown bonsai and use a compost suitable for the tree. Do not over-water for the next two to three weeks, and protect from frost. Allow the tree to gain in health and then feed with a balanced fertiliser to encourage new growth. Root prune every two years from now on; this in time will form a fibrous root system.

Another way of obtaining large specimen trees in a short space of time is to collect from the wild, or buy from a nursery specialising in growing specimen trees, specimens which are already fairly large. This practice is totally the opposite to growing bonsai from seed or cutting because of the reduction in size, and is very similar in technique to growing in the soil except that large growing boxes are used for transplanting. This allows the root system to be reduced slowly over a period of two to three years. Because the thickness and aged appearance is already there, it is just a case of forming the shape you are looking for by training. Jining tends to be used in abundance, mainly to cover the large pruning scars left through drastic pruning. Many English specimen trees are grown this way and 'created' at talks and demonstrations, but before the beginner attempts such things try to find out if the tree which was demonstrated upon is still alive six months later. In most cases you will find the only trees which are still living are those in the hands of the advanced bonsai student who has carefully chosen the tree. The beginner should remember that only on odd occasions can one find or create an instant bonsai.

Specimen Growing Boxes

These are normal, large, wooden boxes with drainage holes at the bottom. Root pruning is kept to a minimum when first transplanting from the wild or from very deep pots, allowing the root system to recover.

PINCHING/DISBUDDING

This technique can be used to control growth and size of needles (see Fig 51), the beginner may try, but mastering the technique on spruce and pine may take several years. Pinching is only one of the factors governing the growth rate; careful watering and feeding also play an important part. Junipers on the other hand are fairly straightforward and should cause no problem to the beginner. The golden rule to remember on all three forms of

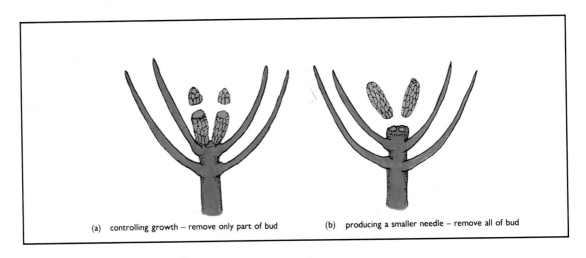

(a) controlling growth – remove only part of bud   (b) producing a smaller needle – remove all of bud

Fig 51 *The beginner should leave pines alone until they have tried the basic principles of disbudding on other forms of trees.*

Fig 52 *Small white pine, 9 years old, ready to start its vigorous needle training.*

bonsai is to use a soft pinch, finger and thumb, and never prune with trimming tools which will damage the foliage and turn it brown. However, it is almost certain that the beginners will experience a little browning of the needles on several of their first attempts.

Pinching Spruce (*Picea jezoensis*)

Young bud growth, rich in colour, starts opening in the spring, with the largest opening first. This process can take between two and three weeks before all the buds are fully opened. During this period, pinching is carried out by starting with the earliest and followed through until the last bud has opened, (see Fig 53). One word of warning before you attempt to pinch; never work on a tree that is unhealthy or under attack from pest or disease.

Step one Never allow the bud to develop fully, always pinch when the bud is half-way or just over half-way.

Step two Grip the bud between your finger and thumb, pinch and pull to remove the bud.

Watering

Never allow the compost to dry out, but at the same time do not allow it to become too wet. Find a balance between the two and keep slightly on the dry side. Keep out of windy conditions and check once a week for needles dropping. Some of the needles will fall through natural processes, but if too many fall there may be several reasons for this, such as having placed the tree in a windy position, allowing it to dry out too quickly, over-watering, or the tree being attacked by an insect. Prune to allow light and air to move freely in the centre of the tree, otherwise these needles will die and drop through lack of light.

Feeding

Feed once a month during the spring (April and May) with a balanced N.P.K. of 7:7:7 plus trace elements and again once a month in August and September with a feed high in phosphate and potash, but low in nitrogen.

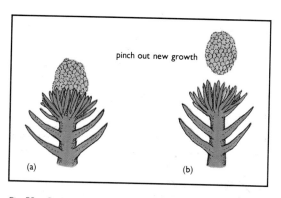

Fig 53 *Disbudding spruce to control growth.*

DISBUDDING PINES

Again I must say that pines are a very specialised subject and there are those who have spent a lifetime studying the pine's growing habits, both pinching buds and controlling the sap flow to form more side branches. The latter is carried out by wounding with a knife just above a bud. However, this is not some mystical practice used on pine trees alone; in fact gardeners have been using this technique in England for a very long time on fruit trees and other shrubs. When disbudding the Japanese White pine (*Pinus Parviflora*), the buds, or 'candles' as they are also termed, can be removed from the white pine during the months of March and April. All the buds can be removed on those trees which have grown long needles or are, as it is termed, 'hairy' but this should only be done every three years and providing the tree is in good health.

Fig 55   New growth on the white pine.

Fig 54   White pine (35 years old), with long needles due to a two year rest period.

White Pine

With finger and thumb, pinch out the bud as in Fig 53. The tree may become slow and sick-looking during the following year, therefore extra care should be given. Watering and feeding is basically the same as for the spruce, but do not over feed and keep the dilution rate slightly below the recommended level stated on the bottle or packet.

Black Pine

Black pine will form a very interesting, aged-looking trunk in a short space of time. The disadvantage, if you can call it one, is the size or the 'hairiness' of the needles. The difference between the black and the white pine is that you can clip the ends of the needles of the black pine, but I must stress that this can only be carried out on the black pine; never attempt to clip the white pine. Some of the needles may turn brown and drop, but new growth will soon replace these.

CHAPTER 6

An A–Z of Trees

The following is a list of trees which can be found in England and you may, if you wish, base your style on the Japanese forms although it is nice to create everyday English shapes modelled on trees found in parks and woodlands. Some of the English trees will not adapt so readily to the bonsai method of growing and this is why the Japanese use maples and other small cultivated trees. The leaves on trees such as oak and horse chestnut tend to be too large for a bonsai tree and therefore will need root and leaf pruning every other year for the first ten to fifteen years.

NAMES

Botanical names can be baffling to the beginner, and many would say they are a waste of time, but a botanical name is an international way of naming a plant, and with the thousands of common names in England alone finding the right tree could become a problem without such an organised system. In this chapter I have tried to overcome the problem by giving the first part of the botanical name followed by a common name; the beginner will soon recognise that *Acer* is a maple and *Fagus* is a beech. This is followed by a species and sometimes a variety or cultivar. To avoid confusion over species, variety and cultivar, I have used words such as 'forms' and 'types'. The experienced plant collectors should bear with us at this point and recall how hard it was to pronounce, yet alone remember, all these names at first.

ACER

There are many forms of *Acer* (maple), most of them originating from Japan. The Japanese maple, *A. palmatum*, is a small, shrub-like tree which is very slow growing and produces a pleasant autumn colour. Other *palmatum* forms, such as *A. palmatum* 'Senkaki' (coral bark maple), with its coral-red branches, gives excellent winter colour. *A. palmatum* 'Dissectum' has a leaf which is divided into five to nine pinnatifid lobes as opposed to *A. palmatum* which has a solid leaf structure. *A. griseum* (paperbark maple), which originated from China, has a bark which flakes to expose a coloured underbark. *A. campestre* (field maple) came from west Asia, but has been growing in England for many years. The autumn colour can be a bright yellow, and sometimes has a red tinge.

A. pseudoplatanus (sycamore) also came from west Asia, but has been grown in this country for a long time and is now classed as an English tree. The leaves on the sycamore tend to be on the large side and again this is one of those trees which will need root and leaf pruning every year.

For all the maples shown below, propagation is by seed, cuttings or grafting.

Tree   *A. campestre* (field maple)
Habit   Deciduous. Medium size, formal style.
Compost   Code 5. Likes heavy compost; do not let the compost become too dry.
Root prune   Every year up to five, then every two to three years.

Fig 56   *Two trident maples, 50 years old.*

Likes   Likes moist conditions.
Pest   Aphids; spray with soapy water.
Disease   Canker, coral spot, die-back, tar spot and powdery mildew.
Wiring   Wire during the growing season, cover wire to protect bark, remove after six months.

Tree   *A. griseum* (paperbark maple)
Habit   Deciduous. Slow growing, trunk flakes to show underbark, most styles.
Compost   Code 3. Open, well drained, sandy compost.
Root prune   Every year up to five, then every two years.
Likes   Part shade or sun. Dislikes wind.
Pest   Aphids; spray with soapy water.
Disease   Canker, coral spot, die-back, tar spot and powdery mildew.

Wiring   During the growing season, cover wire to protect bark, remove after six months.

Tree   *A. grosseri* (snake-bark maple)
Habit   Deciduous. Slow growing, very attractive bark, most styles.
Compost   Code 3. Open, well drained, sandy compost.
Root prune   Every year up to five, then every two years.
Likes   Part shade or sun. Dislikes strong winds.
Pest   Aphids; spray with soapy water.
Disease   Canker, coral spot, die-back, tar spot and powdery mildew.
Wiring   During the growing season, cover wire to protect bark, remove after six months.

Tree   *A. japonicum* 'Aureum'

Habit Deciduous. Slow growing, yellow leaves.

Compost Code 3. Open, well drained, sandy compost.

Root prune Every year up to five, then every two years.

Likes Part shade. Sun will scorch the leaves.

Pest Aphids; spray with soapy water.

Disease Canker, coral spot, die-back, tar spot and powdery mildew.

Wiring During the growing season, cover wire to protect bark, remove after six months.

Tree *A. palmatum* (all types)
Habit Deciduous. Slow growing with good autumn colour, most styles.

Compost Code 3. Open, well drained, sandy compost.

Root prune Every year up to five, then every two or three years.

Likes Part shade. Dislikes strong winds and frost.

Pest Aphids; spray using soapy water.

Disease Canker, coral spot, die-back, tar spot and powdery mildew.

Wiring During the growing season, cover wire to protect bark, remove after six months.

Tree *A. pseudoplatanus* (sycamore)
Habit Deciduous. Large, fairly fast growing tree, formal or informal style.

Compost Code 4. Will tolerate most compost.

Root prune Every year, for the first fifteen years.

Likes Will tolerate part shade or sun.

Pest Aphids; spray with chemical or soapy water.

Disease Canker, coral spot, die-back, tar spot and powdery mildew.

Wiring During the growing season, remove after six months.

Tree *A. platanoides* (Norway maple) 'Crimson King'

Habit Deciduous. Fast growing, hardy, leaves purple-red.

Compost Code 4. Will tolerate most compost.

Root prune Every year up to ten years, then every two years.

Likes Part shade or full sun.

Disease Canker, coral spot, die-back, tar spot and powdery mildew.

Wiring During the growing season, remove after six months.

Acacia See page 98.

AESCULUS

The *Aesculus* (horse chestnut) is one of the most widely-known trees in England. It is

Fig 57   Red maple, 25 years old.

popular with young children for its seed (conkers), which if planted will germinate quite easily and are therefore ideal for the beginner. *Aesculus hippocastanum* is the common horse chestnut and has white flowers in May, but it will take a number of years before it will flower as a bonsai. There are two other forms of the horse chestnut, *A. hippocastanum* 'Pumila' which is a dwarf form with smaller leaves and *A. indica* (Indian horse chestnut) that produces pink-flushed flowers. The leaves on the common and the Indian will need leaf pruning every year to keep them small.

Tree *Aesculus* (all forms)
Habit Deciduous, except for 'Pumila' large trees.
Compost Code 5. Heavy, moist compost with free drainage.
Root prune Every year up to fifteen, then every two years.
Likes Part shade or sun.
Pest Mainly trouble-free.
Disease Coral spot, die-back.
Wiring During the growing season, remove wire after six months.
Propagation Seeds sown in pots or in a prepared site in the garden, or grafting.

ARBUTUS

The *Arbutus* (strawberry tree), a small evergreen, can make an excellent bonsai and with age the trunk and branches of *Arbutus andrachnoides* will transform into a cinnamon-red colour. The tree produces a white flower during late autumn and early winter, followed by a strawberry-like fruit, which is totally unsuitable for eating. The leaves, which are a glossy green, are inclined to be too large for a bonsai tree, therefore you will need to leaf prune over a period of several years to create a smaller leaf.

Tree *A. andrachnoides*
Habit Deciduous. Small, slow growing tree, strawberry-like fruits, colourful bark.
Compost Code 4 or 3.
Root prune Every year up to ten, then every two years.
Likes Sun or part shade.
Pest Mainly free from pest.
Disease Coral spot, die-back.
Wiring During the growing season; cover wire to protect bark, remove after six months.
Propagation Seeds or cuttings.

Azalea See rhododendron.

BETULA

Many people would recognise the *Betula* (silver birch) by the silver bark which gives it its name. *Betula pendula*, which produces the silver bark, makes a good substitute for the Japanese white beech, especially when using it for group planting.

Tree *B. pendula* (common silver birch).
Habit Fast growing tree.
Compost Code 4 or 5, but not too wet.
Root prune Every year up to five, then every two years.
Likes Sun or part shade.
Pest Caterpillars.
Disease Canker, coral spot, die-back.
Wiring During the growing season; cover wire to protect bark, remove after six months.
Propagation Seeds or grafting.

CARPINUS

The *Carpinus* ('Hornbeam') makes an excellent bonsai whether grown as a single bonsai specimen or in a group. *Carpinus betulus* is the common hornbeam and has a sturdy-

Fig 58 Hornbeam, 8 years old.

looking grey trunk, a feature which is very noticeable when grown as a large specimen bonsai. *C. japonica* is a smaller, wide-spreading hornbeam which produces catkins and is probably better suited to bonsai than *C. betulus*.

Tree *Carpinus* ('Hornbeam')
Habit Deciduous. *C. japonica* is slower than *C. butulus*.
Compost Code 4. Will do well in most types of compost.
Root prune Every year up to five, then every two years.
Likes Sun or part shade.
Pest Caterpillar.
Disease Coral spot, die-back, powdery mildew.
Wiring During the growing season, remove after six months.
Propagation Seeds or grafting.

CORNUS

The small, flowering tree *Cornus* (*Cornus-mas*), which is also known as the 'Cornelian Cherry', will make a delightful bonsai, breaking forth to expose its bright yellow flowers on naked branches during the cold, empty months of late winter. The fruits are red and resemble those of a bonsai crab apple.

Tree *Cornus-mas* ('Cornelian Cherry')
Habit Deciduous. Slow growing, forms a net of thick crossing branches.
Compost Code 4. Will do well in most compost.
Root prune Every year up to five, then every two years.
Likes Sun or part shade.
Pest Caterpillars.
Disease Coral spot, die-back.
Wiring Will form a block shape if trained from bud pinching, therefore wire during the growing season; remove after six months.
Propagation Seeds or hardwood cuttings in November.

CRATAEGUS

Crataegus monogyna is the common haw-thorn, which is sometimes called the 'May Tree'. It is one of my favourite bonsai trees. It has fragrant white flowers in May, followed by red fruits in the autumn. Being very hardy it will stand up to most of our cold English winters.

Tree *C. monogyna* (hawthorn)
Habit Deciduous. Slow growing, with thick crossing branches.
Compost Code 5. Will tolerate a wide range of compost.
Root prune Every year up to five, then every two years.
Likes Sun or part shade.
Pest Caterpillars.

Fig 59   Hawthorn, 30 years old.

Disease   Coral spot.
Wiring   During growing season; cover wire to protect bark, remove after six months.
Propagation   Air-layering, simple layering, seed or grafting.

Eucalyptus   *See* indoor section under blue gum (page 100), cider gum (page 101) and lemon (page 106).

FAGUS

Fagus (beech) is one of our old, noble English trees and a favourite among many people collecting English bonsai. *Fagus sylvatica* is the common form of beech and widely used in bonsai; however, there are other forms of beech, such as *F. sylvatica* 'Riversii' which has dark purple leaves. Both have fairly large foliage and need pruning every 1–2 years.

Tree   *F. sylvatica* and *F. sylvatica* 'Riversii'
Habit   Deciduous. Slow growing, prefers a deep pot for root system
Compost   Code 4 or 5. Likes compost low in peat content and well drained.

Root prune   Every year up to five, then every two years.
Likes   Sun or part shade
Pest   Scale insects
Disease   Canker, coral spot, die-back.
Propagation   Seed or grafting.

FRAXINUS

Fraxinus (ash) is very hardy and will tolerate most of our cold winters. *Fraxinus excelsior* is the common ash, easily recognised by its black buds in winter. The leaves are pinnate and tend to start off large, but with a few years of root pruning and leaf pruning they will soon start to take shape. Other forms, such as *F. excelsior* 'Nana', which is more of a bush than a tree, and *F. excelsior* 'Erosa', a small tree with a narrow shaped leaf, make excellent bonsai. Flowering forms such as *F. floribunda*, have large white flowers.

Tree   *F. excelsior* (common ash)
Habit   Deciduous. Hardy, fast growing ('Nana' and 'Erosa', slow growing).
Compost   Code 4 or 5.
Root prune   Every year up to ten, then every two years.
Likes   Sun or part shade.
Pest   Mainly pest free.
Disease   Coral spot, die-back.
Wiring   During growing season; cover wire to protect bark, remove after six months.
Propagation   Seed.

LABURNUM

The small yellow flowering tree *Laburnum* ('Golden Rain') will make an excellent bonsai and will make other bonsai growers very envious when it is in full bloom, late spring to early summer. *Laburnum leguminosae* is the common laburnum but beware, the seeds are poisonous.

Tree *Laburnum leguminosae* ('Golden Rain'), also called 'Golden Shower'
Habit Deciduous. Small, slow growing.
Compost Code 4.
Likes Sun or part shade.
Root prune Every year up to five, then every two years.
Pest Mainly pest free.
Disease Coral spot.
Wiring During growing season; cover wire to protect bark, remove after six months.
Propagation Seeds or hardwood cutting in November.

MALUS

Malus is a small, very hardy flowering crab apple with a thick trunk which produces small cherry-like fruits in the autumn. The leaves and flowers tend to look too large for the tree and will not respond to leaf pruning like other bonsai. *Malus floribunda* or Japanese crab, is the most widely used crab in bonsai and produces crimson buds which open into white flowers early in the spring, followed by red and yellow fruit in the autumn.

Tree *Malus floribunda* (Japanese crab apple)
Habit Deciduous. Small, slow growing tree.
Compost Code 5.
Root prune Every year up to ten, then every two years.
Likes Sun or part shade.
Pest Aphids, caterpillars.
Disease Canker, coral spot, die-back, fire blight, powdery mildew.
Wiring During the growing season; cover wire to protect bark, remove after six months.
Propagation Budding, grafting and seed.

MORUS

This small, slow growing tree is gradually gaining popularity in bonsai circles. *Morus alba* or the white mulberry produces a white fruit which turns to a pinkish-red colour, adding interest to the tree. Although originally from China and not introduced into this country until the fifteenth century, it has become a prized English tree. *M. nigra* is the black mulberry, an excellent tree for bonsai with its wide, spreading top growth and thick, gnarled, old-looking trunk. *M. ruba*, commonly called the red mulberry, is very hard to find in local garden centres and nurseries, but also makes an interesting bonsai. *M. nana* is the slow-growing dwarf form, with very compact top growth which needs constant thinning, but is definitely a tree not to be missed.

Tree *M. alba*, *nana* and *ruba* (mulberries).
Habit Deciduous, slow growing.
Compost Code 3. Open, well-drained compost.

Fig 60 Laburnum, 7 years old.

Root prune Every year up to five, then every two years.
Likes Sun or part shade.
Pest Caterpillars.
Disease Coral spot, die-back.
Wiring During the growing season; remove wire after six months.
Propagation Hardwood cuttings in November.

Myrtus See page 107.
Nandina See under 'Chinese Sacred Bamboo', page 101.

NOTHOFAGUS

Nothofagus antarctica is a fast-growing tree that can make a very attractive bonsai. Commonly known as the antarctic beech, it has small, rounded heart-shaped leaves which turn yellow during the autumn fall.

Tree *N. antarctica.*
Habit Deciduous. Fast growing, will make a good looking tree in a short space of time.
Compost Code 3. Dislikes too much lime.
Root prune Every year up to five, then every two years.
Likes Sun or part shade.
Pest Caterpillars.
Disease Coral spot, die-back.
Wiring During the growing season; cover wire to protect bark, check wire after two months, remove after six months.
Propagation Air-layering, cuttings and seed.

Pomegranate See page 108.

POPULUS

There are many forms of *Populus* (poplar), all of which can be trained into bonsai trees given the time. However, there are a few that have special points of interest and the beginner may wish to try these first. *Populus alba* is the white poplar, because of the white underside of the leaves which turn yellow in the autumn. *P. nigra*, commonly called the black poplar and *P. tremula* 'Pendula', the weeping poplar or weeping aspen, can make a very attractive weeping bonsai.

Tree *P. alba*, *nigra* and *tremula* 'Pendula'
Habit Deciduous.
Compost Code 4.
Root prune Every year up to ten, then every two years.
Likes Sun or shade.
Pest Mainly pest free.
Disease Coral spot.
Wiring During the growing season; remove after six months.
Propagation Hardwood cuttings in November.

Fig 61 Prunus, 10 years old.

PRUNUS

Prunus avium, also called the wild cherry or gean, can be trained into a very attractive and colourful flowering bonsai. Its smooth grey bark will turn red with age; the flowers which blossom in April are white and are followed by small, red to purple fruits.

Tree *P. avium*
Habit Deciduous, slow growing.
Compost Code 4 or 5.
Root prune Every year up to five, then every two years.
Likes Sun or part shade.
Pest Mainly pest free.
Disease Canker, coral spot, die-back.
Wiring During the growing season; cover wire to protect bark, remove after six months.
Propagation Budding, cuttings, grafting, and seed.

Fig 62   Oak, 7 years old.

QUERCUS

The *Quercus* (oak tree) can, given time, form into a small but mighty version of the magnificent specimens seen in the English countryside. However, oaks do not lend themselves too readily to bonsai training. The leaves on the oak tend to be too large and even with the leaf pruning technique you cannot guarantee a smaller leaf, and almost invariably the new leaves that form will be larger than the leaves taken off. The oak will in most cases only live for short periods of time. I have grown some successfully for ten to fifteen years only to find them die overnight, even though they have been given careful attention. Looking back on the losses, some died in prolonged freezing weather conditions, and some in dry, hot summers, even though watering was maintained every day. Others died due to very shallow bonsai pots; it was found that the oaks planted in deep bonsai pots survived longer.

Common Oak *(Q. robur)* English oak.
Cork Oak *(Q. suber)* Corky bark.
Holm Oak *(Q. ilex)* Evergreen oak.
Red Oak *(Q. rubra)* Leaves start green, then turn red before autumn.
White Oak *(Q. alba)* Good autumn colour.
Willow Oak *(Q. phellos)* Willow-like leaves.

Tree Most oaks.
Habit Slow growing, large leaves.
Compost Code 5.
Root prune Every year up to ten, then every two years.
Like Sun or part shade.
Pest Mainly pest free.
Disease Mainly free from disease.
Wiring Try to shape by bud pruning; otherwise wire during the growing season and remove after six months.
Propagation Sow seeds in pots or a prepared plot in the garden during the autumn.

71

RHODODENDRON

Both rhododendron and azalea are linked to the same family, Ericaceae, and the majority tend to be classed as a shrub rather than a tree. There is, however, *Rhododendron arboreum* which forms into a small tree and is suitable for a large, soil grown, specimen bonsai as shown in chapter 5. For growers living in areas where the soil has a high lime content, it would be advisable to grow rhododendron in the specimen training boxes also shown in chapter 5, as rhododendron and azalea will not survive in a compost or a soil that contains lime. They will also need an individual feeding programme as shown in chapter 2. Other forms of rhododendron and azaleas will still make tree-like bonsai (see page 109).

R. arboreum should be grown as a large specimen because the leaves and flowers will look better proportioned than on a smaller version. Even with leaf pruning, the leaves will still be slightly on the large side. As with most rhododendrons R. arboreum will prefer part-shade, and protection from strong winds and frost. Three other names may be added to our list of suitable types:

'Album'   White flowers.
'Blood Red'   Red flowers.
'Roseum'   Pink flower.

Tree   *R. arboreum*, 'Album', 'Blood Red' and 'Roseum'
Habit   Fairly slow growing.
Compost   Code 2 with added feed throughout the growing season.
Root prune   Every two years when grown in soil and boxes, then every year up to five when grown in large bonsai pot, from then on every two to three years.
Likes   Part shade. Dislikes frost, especially 'Blood Red'.
Pest   Rhododendron bug.
Disease   Chlorosis, azalea gall.

Wiring   During the growing season; cover wire to protect bark, remove after six months.
Nursery Stock   Most garden centres will stock or order most rhododendrons and azaleas, but not always at the seedling stage.
Seeds   Sow the seeds between the end of March and the beginning of April in compost code 1, under cover. No heat is required at this time of year except during a very cold spring when a temperature of 13°C (55°F) will be helpful.
Cuttings   Take cutting from the end of July to the first week in September, using compost Code 2. Place the cutting under cover such as a cold frame.
Grafting   Saddle grafting. Not suitable for the beginner.
Layering   See page 28.

ROBINIA

Robinia pseudoacacia (common acacia), also called false acacia and black locust, can be shaped into a colourful, white-flowering bonsai, with a slight scent. The rugged bark is an extra bonus and a bonsai with an aged appearance can be produced in a short space of time.

Tree   R. pseudoacacia
Habit   Slow growing.
Compost   Code 3 or 4.
Root prune   Every year up to five, then every two years.
Pest   Mainly pest free.
Disease   Mainly free from disease.
Wiring   During the growing season; remove wire after six months.
Propagation   Seeds, grafting during March, root cutting taken between December and January.

SALIX

There are many forms of *Salix* (willow), from large weeping trees to small ground cover shrubs. Willows are recognised and accepted when cut back hard (pollarded) and therefore can be modelled on the natural shapes found in the wild. However, there are certain forms which are more suited than others.

S. caprea, commonly called the goat willow or pussy willow, can be shaped into an interesting bonsai with silver catkins which turn to yellow. The stems lend themselves quite readily to bending and shaping with wire, but care should be taken and the wire covered to protect the bark.

S. caprea 'Pendula' is the weeping form and because it is grafted at the top, or 'top worked' as it is termed, it is better for the beginner to purchase a young tree from a nursery or garden centre. They will be sold from about 45cm (18in) high, and are therefore ideal starting material.

S. repens, or creeping willow as it is commonly known, is more of a shrub than a tree, and because of its creeping habit it will make an ideal tree for a cascading bonsai. There are many creeping forms which you may use, such as: *S. argentea* which will need a compost that is moist and sandy such as compost Code 3; *S. repens subopposita* 'Voorthuizen', with very small catkins; *S. reticulata* which again likes moist, open compost such as Code 3.

Tree All *Salix*
Habit Fast growing, ages quickly, upright, weeping and cascade.
Compost Compost Code 3 for most weeping and Code 4 for all others.
Root prune Every year up to five, then every two years.
Pest Aphids, caterpillars.
Disease Die-back, mildew.
Wiring During the growing season; cover wire to protect bark, remove after six months.

Fig 63   *Willow, 30 years old.*

Propagation Very easy from hardwood cuttings taken during November.

SORBUS

The most common of the *Sorbus* is the mountain ash which may also be called the rowan. This tree can make a very interesting flowering bonsai with red fruits and pinnate leaves. Other forms such as the *S. aucuparia* 'Fastigiata', which is very slow growing and has red fruits, will make a good, formal shaped bonsai.

Tree All *Sorbus*
Habit Slow growing, flowering and fruiting.
Compost Code 3 or 4.
Root prune Every year up to five, then every two years.
Likes Sun or part shade.
Pest Mainly free.
Disease Mainly free.
Wiring During the growing season; remove after six months. Do not wire *S. aucuparia* if possible.
Propagation Seeds sown between March and April, grafting during March.

73

STEWARTIA

An excellent tree for bonsai, *Stuartia* has a bark which flakes with age adding to the beauty and charm of this slow growing tree. There are two forms, 'Koreana' and 'Pseudo-camellia' both of which make an excellent bonsai for the beginner, but it is important to remember that they both need a lime-free soil to survive.

Tree   All Stewartia
Habit   Slow growing, interesting bark.
Compost   Code 2 with a feed added at a later stage. See feeding.
Root prune   Every year up to five, then every two years.
Likes   Part shade.
Pest   Mainly pest free.
Disease   Mainly free from disease.
Wiring   During the growing season; cover wire to protect bark, remove after six months.
Propagation   Seeds sown in March, softwood cutting taken in June and placed in coldframe or glasshouse, air-layering between April and July.

SYRINGA

A very common flowering shrub or small tree found in England, *Syringa* (lilac) makes excellent, flowering bonsai, but some are better than others. *Syringa microphylla*, which has small leaves and fragrant flowers, is an excellent form.

Tree   All *Syringa*
Habit   *S. microphylla* is smaller than most others.
Compost   Code 4.
Root prune   Every year up to eight, then every two years.
Likes   Sun or part shade.
Pest   Mainly pest free.
Disease   Mainly free from disease.

Wiring   During the growing season; remove after six months.
Propagation   Seeds sown in March, simple layering April to July, grafting in March under cover.

TILIA

Now that more people are taking an interest in growing their own bonsai from seedlings and seeds, *Tilia* (lime) is steadily growing in popularity. The lime has long been known for its tolerance of heavy pruning, making it an ideal tree for beginners' bonsai training. *Tilia* × *europaea* and *Tilia* × *euchlora* are the most common forms of lime trees and the type used for most roadside plantings. Other forms are *T. cordata* which has small leaves, *T. chinensis*, a small tree with a bark that flakes with age, and *T. japonica*, again with small leaves.

Fig 64   Lime, 8 years old.

Fig 65   Zelkova group, 18 years old.

Tree   All limes
Habit   Fairly slow growing, some with small leaves.
Compost   Code 4.
Root prune   Every year up to six, then every two years.
Likes   Sun or part shade.
Pest   Aphids.
Disease   Mainly free from disease.
Wiring   During the growing season, remove after six months.
Propagating   Simple layering, seed.

ULMUS

Not to be confused with the grey bark elm, which is a *Zelkova* and not an *Ulmus*. The most famous of the *Ulmus* is the English elm, *U. procera* which the adult bonsai grower will remember but not the young bonsai master, it is sad to say, because almost all elms have been wiped out by Dutch elm disease in recent years. However, there are new signs of growth in hedgerows, and many bonsai English elms have survived, making way for new propagation. Other forms of elm such as the *U. parvifolia*, commonly called the Chinese elm or Chinese water elm, will make an excellent bonsai and may be used as semi-coldroom indoor bonsai. Another excellent bonsai which again may be used for semi-coldroom indoor bonsai is the clone, *Ulmus* x *elegantissima* 'Jacqueline Hillier' or 'Jacqueline Elm'.

Tree   All elms
Habit   Fast growing and can make a good bonsai in a short space of time.
Compost   Code 4.

Root prune Every year up to five, then every two years.
Likes Sheltered spot, part shade.
Pest Mainly pest free.
Disease Mainly free from disease.
Wiring During the growing season; cover wire to protect bark, remove after six months.
Propagation Rooted suckers, seed, softwood cuttings.

ZELKOVA

Zelkova serrata (grey bark elm) is the most common form of *Zelkova* used for bonsai and will make an excellent bonsai in a short space of time, not only looking good during the growing season but also making a very interesting, natural-looking tree with its small, fine branch work during the winter period.

Zelkova also lends itself readily to group plantings, as shown in Fig 65. Autumn colour can be either a red or bronze and it is the luck of the draw which colour is produced when the bonsai are grown from seed.

Tree *Z. serrata*
Habit Quick growing, forming an interesting bonsai in a short space of time.
Compost Code 4 or 5.
Root prune Every year up to five, then every two years.
Pest Mainly pest free.
Disease Mainly free from disease.
Wiring During the growing season; remove after six months.
Propagation Seeds sown between March and April, soft or semi-ripe cuttings, air-layering between April and the end of July.

Fig 65(a) Zelkova, 50 years plus.

Fig 65(b) A small maple group, 18 years old, just entering its dormant season.

CHAPTER 7

Group Plantings

There are four styles which look like group plantings. True group plantings are made up of all individual trees; bonsai landscaped, termed 'Bonkei', is an art form using bonsai to create landscapes; raft uses one continuous base with upright multiple growth; and multiple trunk consists of several trunks arising from one root system.

TRUE GROUP

In both bonsai and horticulture practice, odd numbers are used for group plantings. You may if you wish use even numbers, but you will find odd numbers more effective when creating an informal group, rather than a rigid, straight-lined, formal effect, as illustrated with the *Zelkova* group in Fig 65.

We are looking for an optical illusion, and there are two ways of creating it. Firstly there

Fig 66 *Larger trees at the front will give the optical illusion of depth.*

is the railway line effect; you may remember this from art class at school – the width at the front appears to converge in the distance, as shown in Fig 66. To create this effect, you will need one large tree at the front of your group, behind which are trees of decreasing height.

The second effect you can create is to place one very tall tree in the centre, then plant from the centre outward towards the rim of the pot with trees of decreasing height (Fig 67). The dish is an important factor in group planting, and many shapes and sizes are used, most of them very shallow. This also adds to the illusion.

Individual Tree Group

Step one Choose a suitable pot or tray, but before preparing the mesh, gravel and compost take a look at Fig 68(a). Here you will see a framework made up of either thin bamboo canes or thick training wire. This frame is used to tie the individual trees into the very shallow dish used for the group planting. By using such a frame, you are not restricted to only placing the trees close to drainage holes, which would otherwise be the only way to wire the groups into position. Once you have made your frame, place it at the bottom of the pot and secure it with wire that is pushed through the drainage holes and the mesh. Having done this, secure pieces of wire to the frame at the position where you will place your trees. Then continue to fill the bottom of the dish with 6mm gravel as you would for re-potting.

The trees used should have been chosen prior to planting for their size and shape, such as a tall, straight tree with a clean trunk, another smaller tree with its main growth of branches to the right and one with its branches to the left (see Fig 68(b)). If you have not already done so, draw a plan of how and where you will plant your trees, choosing a back and front also. Try as far as possible to show every tree trunk in the group.

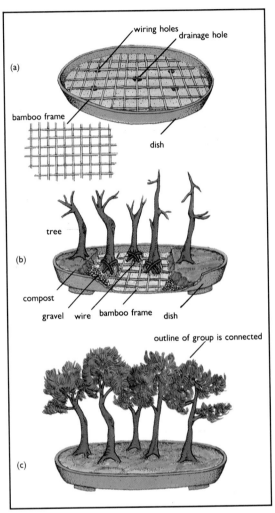

Fig 68 Tying the trees to the cane grid will help to stabilise the trees until they become established.

Step two Once you have secured the mesh and covered it with gravel, lightly cover the gravel with compost as for normal re-potting. Place your trees in the same position as shown on your plan and tie in each tree with the wire that has been secured to the frame (Fig 68(b)).

Cover the root systems with compost, then carefully work the compost down into the root area with a chopstick or dibber. Remember

Fig 67 Two ways of creating an optical illusion of depth: planting a tall tree in the centre and using a shallow dish.

78

raft as group

fallen tree raft

Fig 69   The raft can create the illusion of a clump of trees growing in a group, or give the impression of a fallen tree which has taken root.

the importance of mixing the compost into the root system. You should now have the beginnings of a group planting. The after-care, pruning and wiring is basically the same as for an individual tree, except that the shape of the tree should blend with the rest of the group.

RAFT

The raft is basically one long trunk placed on its side, thus allowing the side branches to grow either as individual trees if creating a

group effect of a multiple trunk with a long woody base, or to give the illusion of a fallen tree that is still growing, as shown in Fig 69. There are two ways to produce a raft, firstly by pot growing and secondly by layering.

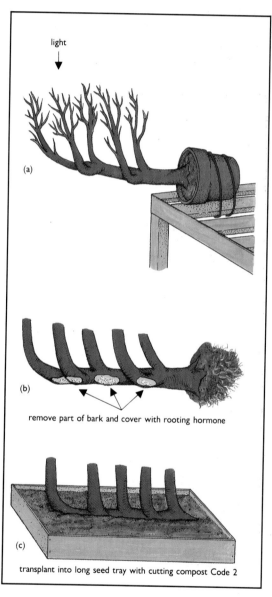

light

(a)

(b)

remove part of bark and cover with rooting hormone

(c)

transplant into long seed tray with cutting compost Code 2

Fig 70   For a pot grown raft, make sure that the pot does not dry out when it is tied on its side to the bench.

79

Pot Grown Raft

Step one Find a pot grown seedling; choose the side which is to produce the growth and prune all the branches from the opposite side, or as we term it the 'under-side'. The pot is then laid on its side and secured to the bench with the growth area facing toward the light as shown in Fig 70(a). Remember to tilt the pot on an angle and cut away part of the pot to allow for watering.

Step two Now think through the design and individual tree or branch shapes you wish to create, and draw a plan to use for future reference. For the next growing season, leave the pot tied to the bench and continue to train the raft into the desired shapes. During the spring of the following year, remove a small section on the under-side of the main trunk. Cover these sections with a rooting hormone and transplant into a long, deep seed tray with 6mm gravel placed at the bottom, then covered with compost Code 2 (Fig 70(b) and (c)).

Step three Do not root prune for the next three years. Remove some of the compost from the surface and replace with fresh compost. Continue to train the top section of the raft and feed after the first month but remember that Code 2 is a cutting compost, low in nutrients, and therefore feeding is a very important factor. Water as you would for normal bonsai. During the spring of the fourth year, remove from the seed tray, root prune and transplant into a long bonsai dish.

Layering

A stem which has been layered and allowed to develop a continuous root system, such as the one in 'continuous layering', should be anchored into a training seed tray with 6mm gravel placed on the bottom with Code 2 used for the compost, as shown in Fig 71. Feed and

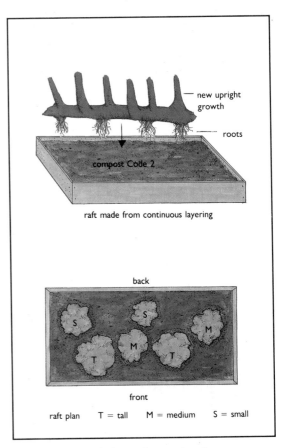

raft made from continuous layering

raft plan   T = tall   M = medium   S = small

Fig 71   *It is a good idea to draw a plan of the expected result to guide you.*

water the same as you would for pot grown raft. As with the pot grown raft, draw a plan that will show the end result; this will save time and mistakes.

MULTIPLE TRUNK

This formation is a tree with several trunks extending from the root base, as shown in Fig 72. Odd numbers will give the best results. Each trunk is treated as an individual but at the same time the top growth should blend together as one unit.

Fig 72   *The multiple trunk extends from one root base.*

LANDSCAPE (BONKEI)

This is an art on its own, very similar to growing bonsai groups except rocks, water, houses and bridges are used (See Fig 73). The shape of the dish you use depends on the style and effect you are trying to create. Drainage is just as important with landscapes as it is with any other bonsai, therefore mesh and gravel are still used when potting. Wiring trees in position or using a frame made of thin bamboo or thick training wire may be necessary when using shallow dishes.

Rocks

Never use such items as house bricks or pieces of concrete for rocks. Thermal blocks are used by several bonsai clubs, mainly because they are easy to carve into shapes,

Fig 73   *A small landscape with rocks, a house and water.*

and because they are porous. Another way to find rock is simply to visit the countryside, go on cliff walks, or obtain permission to visit a local quarry. Try to pick a rock that has plenty of interest, and which is flat at the bottom if possible, as this will help stabilise it when in the dish. If two rocks are used, try to match them up so that it looks like one piece of rock instead of two. Drill holes in the bottom of the rock if it is top heavy. Wire can be pushed through these holes, to anchor the rock to the dish.

Slate

Groups look very effective when planted on a flat piece of slate. To make such a group you must first drill holes through the slate, as shown in Fig 74(a). Wire is then pushed through the holes (Fig 74(b)). The trees are

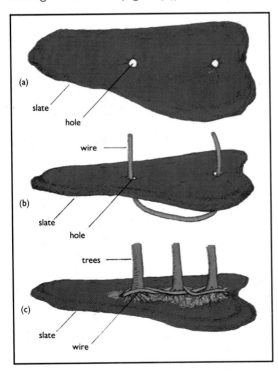

Fig 74 Keep a check on the watering when planting over slate and keep out of strong winds.

placed in position and wired to the slate (Fig 74(c)).

The type of compost used for growing on slate should have plenty of water retention. Therefore use extra moss peat mixed with sphagnum moss, which can be purchased from your local garden centre or florist shop. Compost is spread over the root system, working the compost in between the roots and finally covering the complete root area.

The experienced bonsai grower will make this technique look very easy, growing groups and single trees on very small and flat pieces of slate, but for the beginner it would be better to pick a piece of slate that has a hollow, or an angled shape, to sit the trees in.

Moss

To stop the compost from being washed away moss, like that which grows around the bottom of trees in woods or over stone walls, is encouraged to grow over the compost. Another method is to place a very fine hair net over the compost and pin it at the sides. Moss is then pushed into the compost at several points and soon spreads, covering and disguising the net.

Make sure when collecting moss that it is free from pest, disease and chemical contamination. Moss collected from the lawn may have traces of weedkiller in it, and moss found around the base of tree roots may have a brushwood weedkiller on it. The safest way, therefore, is to grow your own.

To grow your own moss you will need a container such as a seed tray with a few drainage holes. Place old compost left over after re-potting into the tray, adding more moss peat to the compost if it is Code 3 or lower. Place the tray in a shady part of the garden, water it regularly and the moss will grow.

NOTE So that you will not become confused which type of moss is being used, we

Fig 75   A very young juniper, 3 years old, planted on a piece of slate.

Fig 76   The same juniper, showing how it is wired to the piece of slate.

will term the moss found growing on walls and tree roots 'green moss'. The types of moss to be used are: moss peat (used in the compost); sphagnum moss (helps to hold moisture when mixed with moss peat); and green moss (to help hold the compost on to rocks and also used to give a grass effect under the tree).

Water

The illusion of water can be very effective in a bonkei landscape, and glazed dishes can be purchased with a blue base to create such an illusion. A single landscape on rock filled with water, can give you many hours of pleasure and meditation.

After-Care

Always keep groups or single trees grown on slate out of strong winds and frost. If the small amount of compost is allowed to dry out or freeze, fatal damage will occur to the root system. Water two or three times a day during hot, sunny spells and feed every two weeks throughout the growing season.

Fig 76(a)   Note in this photograph how the rock and water blend together to create an optical illusion. By adding a tree you have the complete bonsai landscape.

CHAPTER 8

Rock Plantings

There are four ways to grow a bonsai tree over rock: straddling the rock with roots; drilling holes to plant the tree; pinning the tree to the rock; and planting next to the rock.

ROCKS

Tufa Rock

Tufa is a very soft rock used by many people in the gardening world to grow a wide range of plants. Holes are cut out very easily with a chisel, and then shaped to fit the root of the bonsai which can spread out inside the rock. The main problem with using tufa for bonsai is that it will not last for very long. As the root system spreads through the rock, cracks will form and eventually the rock will split into several pieces.

Volcanic Rock

Most of the rock you will see in bonsai nurseries is volcanic rock (Fig 77). The rock imported from Japan is very hard and spe-

Fig 77   Treated volcanic rock standing in a tray. Note the stream running down from the mountains.

cially treated to bring out the white, blue, grey and, occasionally, green colours. Such rock can be very costly.

Scottish and Welsh Rock

Some of the rocks found in Scotland and Wales are ideal for growing a root over rock and will cost far less than those which are imported. But remember, before collecting the rock obtain permission first. Once you have collected your rock, wash it several times with boiling water to make sure it is not contaminated in any way.

STRADDLING THE ROCK

This is where the root system sits over the top of the rock as shown in Fig 49. There are many trees which lend themselves to growing over rock, but the best one from the list of trees is the trident maple. Its roots expand very quickly around the rock, biting into the crevice and holding the tree in position.

Step one Find or purchase a piece of suitable rock, looking first at its shape then for a crevice; the rock should have a flat bottom if possible. When choosing your tree, look for a

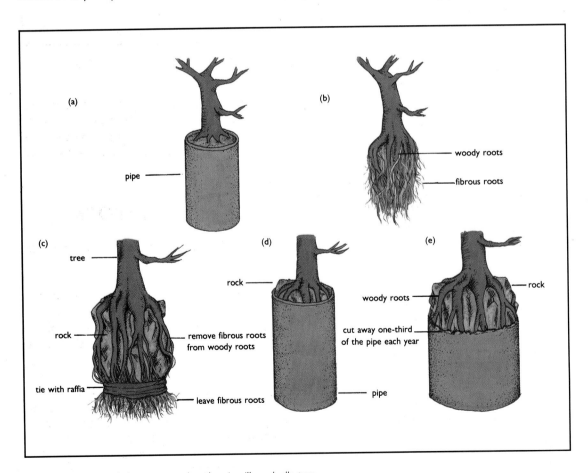

Fig 78   The roots which are exposed to the air will gradually turn woody and expand in the crevice of rock which in turn will hold the tree in place.

86

top shape that balances with your piece of rock and with a 'V' shaped root system. A young tree still in its seedling stage, about two years old, that has not had its tap root cut, is best for the beginner to start with.

Step two During March place the tree into a deep training pot such as an old piece of pipe, in gravel and a sandy compost Code 2, exposing the neck of the root system as shown in Fig 78(a). Leave it in this pot for one season to produce a long root system which is fibrous at the bottom. Continue to prune and shape the top of the tree as normal.

Step three The following March, remove the tree from its pipe. You should find a long fibrous root system with thick roots (Fig 78 (b)); the thick roots are the ones which will sit in the crevice. Pull them apart and separate the thick ones from the root ball. Clean the top part of the thick root.

Step four Carefully place the tree over the top of the rock, straddling the neck of the roots over the rock (See Fig 78(c)). At the same time push the thick roots prepared in step three into the rock's crevice. Tie with raffia or wire to hold the roots in place, then re-pot the tree back into a deep piece of drainage pipe. (Fig 78(d)). For the next two years, carefully remove the compost by one third, cutting the pipe away at the same time (see Fig 78(e)). As soon as the roots are exposed to the air they will begin to turn woody and start to thicken.

Step five After three years you should find that the root system has encased the bottom of the rock and formed a root ball the same shape as the pot. Carefully remove the tree and rock from the pipe; this should come out as one unit. As with normal root pruning, very carefully loosen the root with a chopstick or dibber, starting from the sides and working down to the bottom. Remove any wire or old raffia left from tying the roots to the rock.

Fig 79   Roots exposed over a rock can give a good aged appearance to the tree.

Step six Choose a bonsai pot. The beginner should start with a fairly deep pot and work down to a shallow one over the next three or four years. Re-pot as you would for normal bonsai.

TREES PLANTED IN ROCK

With this type of rock planting we use the rock as a pot.

Step one The rock is the most important item, therefore pick a rock for its shape, a flat base, and interesting features and colour. Remember that tufa rock will only last until the root out-grows the rock.

Step two Mark the two areas you wish to drill, one for the tree's hole and the second for drainage. With a long drill bit, drill a hole through the rock from the top marked area to the bottom marked area as shown in Fig 80(a) and (b).

Step three Continue to drill several smaller

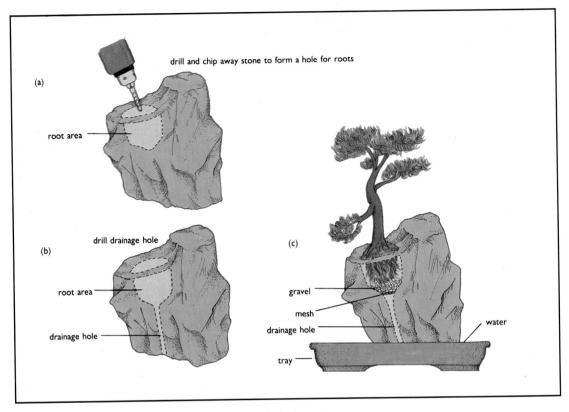

Fig 80   When planting trees in rock, the gravel and mesh will stop the compost from blocking the drainage passage.

holes next to the top hole in a circle, but only to the depth of the root system of the tree being used. Chip away the rock in between the holes to form a pocket to sit the roots in.

Step four   Place a small piece of mesh inside the stone over the drainage hole, then add a thin layer of gravel over the mesh to stop the compost from blocking this hole. Carefully place the root system inside the pocket and work a compost with high water retention into the root area, as in Fig 80(c).

Step five   Choose the pot or tray. A tray without drainage holes and with a blue glazed bottom is ideal. The rock stands in the centre of the tray, which is then filled with water, giving the illusion of a lake or sea.

After-Care

Keep the tree out of strong winds, heavy rain and frost. Never allow the compost to dry out and remember always to water with a fine rose on your watering can. Feed every three weeks during the growing season.

TREES PINNED TO ROCK

Pinning a tree to a rock is very similar to growing a tree on slate, except that this practice is used for those rocks which are too thick to drill.

Step one   Find a suitable rock; one that has a shelf-like top or side, as shown in Fig 81(a).

Step two   Thin training wire is to be pinned with small, thin tacking nails to the rock, so first mark the area where the pins are to go, then with a fine drill bit the same size as the pin, drill a hole. Force the pin into the hole, making sure the fit is tight (see Fig 81(a) and (b)).

Step three   Place the tree in position on the rock, then start winding the wire around pin 1, pulling it across the tree's roots to pin 2, back over to pin 3 and finishing at pin 4, as shown in Fig 81(b) and (c).

Step four   Work compost, extra moss peat and sphagnum moss into the root area. Place a fine hair-net over the compost to help hold the soil, then cover with green moss.

Pot or Tray

A pot or tray can be used, but a very shallow tray filled with water or sand is the most effective. Make sure when using a shallow tray that the bottom part of the stone stands firm.

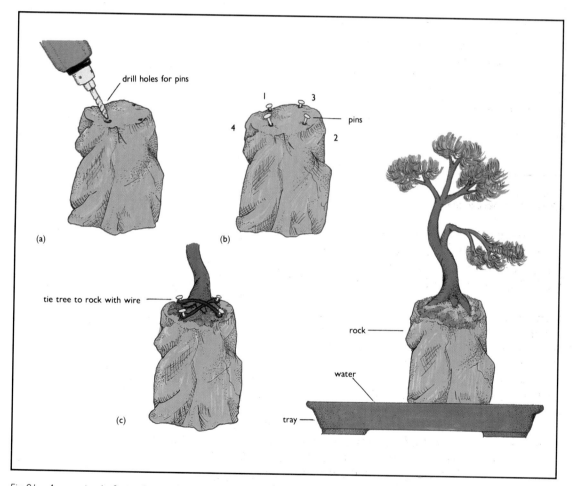

Fig 81   A very simple form of pinning the tree to a rock. Care should be taken never to allow the compost to dry out.

89

Fig 82   Small needle juniper, 7 years old, planted next to a rock.

After-Care

Keep out of strong wind and frost. Never allow the compost to become too dry and feed every three weeks throughout the growing season.

PLANTING NEXT TO A ROCK

There is no technical skill involved in this practice, other than finding a rock which will harmonise with the tree. You may if you wish push a root or two into one of the crevasses, which in time will thicken and force itself to grow around the rock, but otherwise it is basically a matter of positioning the rock when you re-pot the tree, as shown in Fig 82.

Fig 82(a)   An old hawthorn taken from the wild, displayed with a volcanic rock. Note the ruggedness of the pot which gives the final balance

Fig 82(b)   A growing cage (shadery) will help to keep off strong winds and offers some protection from frost.

CHAPTER 9

Indoor Bonsai

Many peoples' idea of a bonsai tree is of a genetically small tree, identical in shape and form to large woodland trees but growing in the living room, nine times out of ten on top of the television. Then comes the realisation that there is no such thing as a genetic bonsai, only normal trees that need time, patience and understanding to grow; also that most bonsai will *only* grow out of doors. There are, however, sub-tropical and tropical trees, all needing the same training programme as the hardy, which would soon die if placed outside in the British climate and it is these trees we term 'indoor bonsai'.

LESS HARDY INDOOR BONSAI

These are trees in between hardy outdoor and sensitive indoor bonsai. Trees such as acacia, azalea, variegated cotoneaster, pistachio, pomegranate, olive (*Olea*), cherry (*Prunus*), monkey puzzle (*Araucaria araucana*) and some forms of elm (*Ulmus*), especially the tender variegated forms, all need a well-lit position in a fairly cool, frost free room with a temperature between 10–20°C (50–70°F). There are exceptions; pomegranate and acacia will tolerate higher temperatures than this.

TRUE INDOOR BONSAI

Lemon tree (*Citrus limon*), kowhai (*Sophora tetraptera*) are the kind of trees used for true indoor bonsai. Before attempting to grow your

indoor bonsai, read through the list of indoor bonsai which describes their likes and dislikes and also through the general rules on keeping them. Then start from step one to learn how to grow an indoor bonsai.

Fig 83   Chinese water elm, 15 years old, a semi-indoor or cold room bonsai.

ENVIRONMENTAL FACTORS

Light and Temperature

These are the two governing factors which allow you to grow bonsai indoors. If the tree is placed in a dark corner of the room several things can happen:

1 The tree will become tall and leggy, which means long spaces will develop between one set of leaves and the next.
2 Photosynthesis, the process by which the tree manufactures vital sugar and starches through its leaves, is slowed down due to the lack of light.
3 The growing tip can turn black, not to be confused with frost damage.

A balanced temperature between 10–18°C (50–64°F) should be maintained at all times; during the summer it should be between 16–18°C (61–64°F) and in winter temperatures should never fall below 10°C (50°F), although some bonsai will tolerate lower temperatures for very short periods. This is a rough guide, and in time you will learn the correct temperature (see *also* individual specifications for each tree in the following lists). Never place the bonsai over any source of uncontrollable heat, such as radiators, or electrical appliances that give off heat. Placing your bonsai in such a position will cause hot soil, which can cause the woody parts of the tree to develop heat canker.

Watering

Never allow the bonsai to dry out completely, always water from the top of the pot and never stand the base of the pot in water for periods of thirty minutes or more, otherwise you will hinder the circulation of air from the top of the pot to the bottom. A humidity tray as illustrated in Fig 84 is ideal, provided the tree is raised above the level of the water. As far as possible use rain water from a clean butt. If this is not available, use boiled tap water that has been standing for more than twenty-four hours.

Feeding

A good feeding programme with a balanced fertiliser containing N.P.K. of 7:7:7, alternating with a tomato feed every two to three weeks depending on the rate of growth, will keep the tree in good health. Never over-feed your bonsai.

Pests and Diseases

Follow a spraying programme for pests and diseases. Pests such as red spider mite (*Tetranychus urticae*), whitefly (*Trialeurodes vaporariorum*) and diseases such as mildews and rots should all be sprayed against.

Fig 84   A humidity tray without drainage holes.

Fig 85   Serissa, 9 years old.

GROWING INDOOR BONSAI

Finding young seedling material for indoor bonsai is more difficult than it is for the hardy outdoor bonsai seedling. It is very doubtful whether they will be available at your local garden centre, unless you are fortunate to live close to a nursery which specialises in house plants. Therefore either visit a bonsai centre or grow from seeds and cuttings. To grow from seed, follow the steps for growing seed indoors described in chapter 3. To grow from cuttings, read through the cutting section for soft and semi-ripe cuttings in chapter 3. Growing from seed or cuttings will take up to five years to produce something that looks like a bonsai.

Year One

Step one (seed)   Once the seeds have been germinated, prick them out into individual pots. Care should be taken not to damage the young shoots and roots when removing them from the compost. Try to lift the seedling by first taking hold of one seed leaf (the leaves which develop before the true leaves) with your finger and thumb, then lift the roots and compost and transplant them, making a hole with a dibber, into a Code 3 or 4 compost, according to whether the tree likes an acid or a neutral compost. Do not prune the roots this year.

Step one (cuttings)   Once the cuttings have taken root, remove them carefully from the cutting compost and transplant them into the seedling Code 3 or 4 compost, again depending on whether the tree prefers an acid or a neutral compost as in the cutting section.

Step two (seedlings from seed and cuttings)   Keep the room temperature between 16–18°C (61–64°F) and give the seedling as much light as possible, but not strong sunlight, turning the seedling to ensure that it receives light from all sides to give it a balanced growth pattern.

Watering and feeding   Do not feed for the first two weeks after transplanting and never allow the compost to become waterlogged. After two weeks, plan a feeding programme using the fertilisers talked about at the beginning of the chapter. Water before the compost becomes completely dry, or as a general rule every other day. Mist over the foliage if the atmosphere becomes dry, or every day if the plant is kept in a room with gas central heating, and every other two days with other types of heating.

Step three   Pinching, pruning and wiring is basically the same as in the training of hardy

Fig 86 *Pistachio, 9 years old.*

door bonsai, basically because of their warmer conditions and the frost-free growing area. Therefore, with the exception of the flowering period, root pruning can take place at almost any time during the year, although it is far better to stick to a planned root pruning programme. The time of year I choose is March to April and September to October, favouring March to April as the best time of the year. I have chosen this time of year because the seed or cutting sown or taken in the previous spring should now be one year old, and this is the time of year when all the other hardy bonsai need re-potting. It is a good idea to keep a yearly record not only of root pruning, but also feeding and spraying. This will ensure you do not root prune twice, or over-feed.

Fig 87 **Pruning Indoor Bonsai.** *(a) Serissa unpruned.*

outdoor bonsai, except that the outdoor bonsai growth slows down during late summer whereas the indoor bonsai growth will slow down slightly but continue *through-out* the year which means constant attention.

Wiring Do not over-wire your tree during the first year; try to shape from buds as far as possible. If you do have to wire in the first year, make sure the branch is woody and not green and sappy otherwise the wire will cut and damage the bark, leaving it open and exposed to diseases. Cover wire with raffia for all trees during the first two years.

Step four (root pruning) Indoor bonsai is not governed by the same rules as the out-

94

(b)   Cutting back new growth.

(c)   Serissa after pruning.

Root prune (March/April year 2) Remove the tree from its pot and take one third of the roots off, the same way you would root prune the hardy bonsai.

After-Care

Careful watering is required over the next two weeks; do not feed for two weeks and keep out of direct sunlight and off cold window ledges.

Continue to train for the next four years using the same techniques, shaping from buds, wiring, taking out crossing branches, as in the hardy bonsai training. After the five year period, the tree can be placed into a decorative bonsai pot if you have not already done so.

Pots

The pot for the indoor bonsai can be glazed outside, but not inside. Large drainage holes are again very important to stop the compost from becoming waterlogged. Frost-proof pots are not essential. Colourful decorative pots with patterns of Japanese or Chinese dragons, landscapes, birds and trees will add to the charm of an indoor bonsai.

Display

How and where you place your bonsai inside the house will not only affect the tree's growth and health, a good choice can also add to the charm and grace of the bonsai. First let us look at where not to place your bonsai.

Fig 88 *A decorative pot adds to the charm of an indoor bonsai.*

Bad Positions

1   Never place your tree on top of the television as heat that is given off may reach very high levels, and the forms of radiation and light it produces may damage the bonsai's growth.

2   Keep bonsai out of rooms with very high temperatures. Read through the indoor bonsai list and find the ideal temperature for each tree.

3   Do not place bonsai on wall units unless there is ample natural light; if lights are fitted to the wall unit then change them for a 'grow light'. (Seek professional advice from an electrician before attempting to fit grow lights to any form of unit.)

4   Keep bonsai out of dark corners in general.

5   Never place your bonsai close to a smokey, open fire.

Good Positions

1   Conservatories are the ideal areas, provided the temperature is not too high and there is good ventilation.

2   Bay windows are again ideal, but the bonsai will need turning from back to front every other day to produce a balanced growth.

3   A large window with patio doors is a good spot; here the tree can receive light and ventilation on warm days. With such a position, a stand such as the ones shown in Fig 89 would add to the effect.

4   For the very keen indoor bonsai grower, a large fish tank fitted with a grow light, temperature control and a fan for ventilation can be used (see Fig 90).

5   A window-ledge has its good and bad points; provided you shade from direct sunlight and remove during the cold nights there should be no problem.

TYPES OF INDOOR BONSAI

Many of the indoor bonsai listed below will be unknown to the beginner, most of them coming from warmer countries. Unlike the hardy bonsai which tends to have a pool of propagation material, the first indoor tree is usually grown from seed. Some of the seeds are temperamental, but they are worth the time and effort.

In the following list, the common names come first and the botanical names second. This is because most of the seeds sold for bonsai are only labelled with the common name. The list contains only a few of the hundreds of trees suitable for indoor bonsai, as you will find out if you study the subject of bonsai in more depth. However, I feel I have listed more than enough to be going on with.

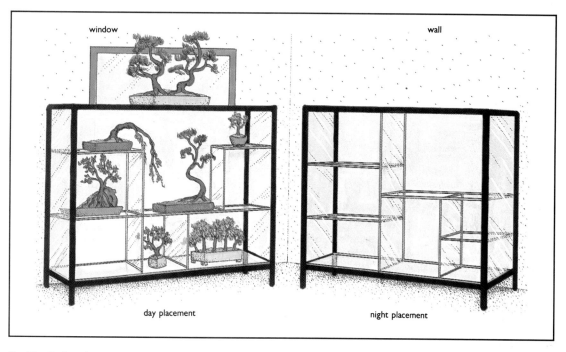

Fig 89   Shelves for the indoor bonsai can be made to look attractive and blend in with other furniture. Trees are moved to night placement to protect from frost during the winter.

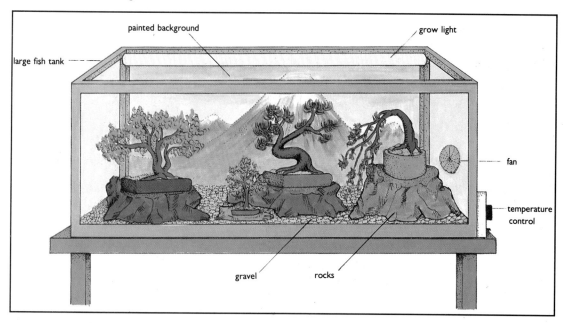

Fig 90   With a fish tank you can create a landscape in miniature.

Note In the following list the words 'Mainly free' are sometimes used when referring to bonsais' susceptibility to pest and disease; however, this does not mean that these bonsai are totally free at all times, merely that they are less troublesome.

FLOWERING AND FRUITING BONSAI

As I have said, bonsai is a mechanical process and not a genetic one, therefore the flowers and fruit will quite often be of normal size. To allow full size fruit to be produced may cause untold damage through sheer weight alone. Therefore, it would be better to remove the fruit before it grows. Removing the flower head before the fruit forms and sets

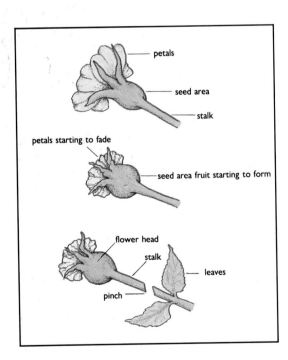

Fig 91 *Removing the flower heads will avoid damaging the fine branch work by stopping the fruit from developing, which would eventually break the branch due to its size and weight.*

seed can be an advantage to the bonsai by pushing all the energy back into the tree. This is almost the same principle as dead heading a rose. Allow the bonsai to flower, but keep an eye on the petals. As soon as they start to fade remove the flower with a piece of the stalk as shown in Fig 91.

ACACIA

The *Acacia karoo* is a yellow-flowering, deciduous tree with fern-like leaves and white thorns. It will make an excellent indoor bonsai. Coming from South Africa it will tolerate the warmer conditions of indoor cultivation.

Position Plenty of light and good ventilation.
Temperature In winter never below 4°C (39°F).
Propagation Seed or cuttings.
Seed Sow seeds in April in compost Code 1, at a temperature of 16°C (61°F).
Cuttings A young, semi-ripe cutting with a heel between the months of April and May, in a compost Code 2 at a temperature between 16–18°C (61–64°F).
Compost Code 4.
Root prune Every year up to five, then every two years.
Pest Mealybug, caterpillars.
Disease Wilt, die-back.

Azalea See rhododendron.

BANANA

Musa taiwan is a deciduous dwarf banana tree from China. To produce the fruit for showing you would need to grow a large specimen bonsai; therefore this is not a tree for the beginner. A small form from the Canary Islands is *M. cavendisbii / M. acuminata* or 'Dwarf Cavendish'.

Fig 92 An indoor group of Serissa.

Position Light shade from May to August. Full light in winter.
Temperature Never allow the temperature to drop below 10°C (50°F) during the winter. In summer keep the temperature below 21°C (70°F).
Propagation Sow seed in April in a compost Code 1, with a temperature of 21°C (70°F).
Compost Code 4.
Root prune Every two to three years. Not a tree for the beginner, can be troublesome.
Pest Red spider mite.
Disease Mildew, allow for ventilation.

BAOBAB

The Baobab (*Adansonia digitata*) is a very large, deciduous tree found in parts of Africa, famous for its trunk which is shaped like a bottle. It is said that this tree can live to a great age. This is not a bonsai for the beginner, but will make a good bonsai to add to anyone's collection.

Position Plenty of light, good ventilation.
Temperature Between 16–18°C (61–64°F).
Propagation Seed sown in April in a compost Code 1, with a temperature of 21°F (70°F).
Compost Code 4.
Root prune Every year up to five, then every two to three years.
Pest Red spider mite.
Disease Wilt, mildew. Allow air to flow freely around the bonsai.

BARBADOS CHERRY

Interesting evergreen trees from the West Indies, the Barbados cherry *Malpighia glabra* and *M. coccigera* can be trained into a delightful bonsai which produces pink flowers.

Position   Plenty of light but not direct sunlight.
Temperature   Should not drop below 18°C (64°F) and never go above 24°C (75°F).
Propagation   Seed and cuttings.
Seed   April in a compost Code 1, with a temperature of 21°C (70°F).
Cuttings   April, softwood cuttings in compost Code 2, bottom heat between 21–25°C (70–77°F).
Compost   Code 4.
Pest   Aphids, red spider mite.
Disease   Mainly free, but prune to allow light and air into the centre of the tree.

BLUE GUM

The tender evergreen tree from Tasmania, blue gum (*Eucalyptus globulus*), will make attractive, colourful, indoor bonsai. It is used by some gardeners as a bedding plant during the summer months, therefore they are available from local nurseries. Its blue-white smooth bark adds to the attraction of this interesting bonsai with white flowers and large black fruits.

Position   Plenty of light and full sun, place outside on warm days during the summer.
Temperature   Cold room with a temperature about 16°C (61°F).
Propagation   Seed sown in February to March in compost Code 1, with a temperature of 13–16°C (55–61°F); cover seed tray with a propagator top.
Compost   Code 4, keep compost moist during the summer months.
Root prune   Carefully root prune every two to four years then every three. Roots can be temperamental when pruned.
Pest   Mainly pest free.
Disease   Mainly free from disease.

For other eucalyptus, see cider gum and lemon.

CARMONA

Carmona (*Carmona microphylla*) is an evergreen shrub with a white flower followed by a berry, reddish in colour. Very tree-like without too much training.

Position   Plenty of light, but not direct sun.
Temperature   Between 15–24°C (59–75°F).
Compost   Code 4.
Propagation   Seed and cuttings.
Seed   Sow seeds in compost Code 1, at a temperature between 16–18°C (61–64°F).
Cuttings   Soft wood or semi-ripe in compost Code 2, at a temperature of 18°C (64°F).
Root prune   Every year up to five, then every two years.
Pest   Aphids, red spider mite.
Disease   Die-back, wilt.

CAROB

The common name for Carob (*Ceratonia siliqua*), an evergreen tree, is 'St John's Bread'. Very easy to grow, it is an ideal indoor bonsai for the beginner.

Position   Plenty of light.
Temperature   Between 16–18°C (61–64°F).
Propagation   Seed, sown in compost Code 1, with a temperature of 16°C (61°F).
Compost   Code 4.
Root prune   Every year up to five, then every two years.
Pest   Mainly pest free.
Disease   Mainly free from disease.

Fig 93   Chinese sacred bamboo, 7 years old.

CHINESE SACRED BAMBOO

The sacred bamboo (*Nandina domestica*) is a small shrub from China, and given time it will form into a cold room flowering bonsai. The flowers are white and show themselves during the month of July. This is followed by a white fruit in August. This is really a semi-indoor bonsai and therefore will need a rest period through the winter. Its advantage is the autumn colour it displays just before the bonsai drops some of its old foliage.

Position   Cool room, but frost free. Plenty of light during the winter and summer and good ventilation.
Temperature   Winter temperature 10°C (50°F), but will tolerate lower temperatures. Summer temperature between 16–18°C (61–64°F).
Propagation   Seed and cuttings.
Seed   Seeds are sown in seed trays and placed outside to over-winter in compost Code 1, without artificial heat.

Cuttings   Treat them the same as a hard-wood cutting, but place in a pot or tray and then in a coldframe or glasshouse.
Compost   Code 4.
Root prune   Every year up to five, then every two years.
Pest   Mainly pest free.
Disease   Mainly trouble free, but prune to allow light and air into the centre of the tree.

CIDER GUM

Cider gum (*Eucalyptus gunnii*) is found in the southern areas of Australia and also grown in parts of England. This evergreen eucalyptus is classed as a cold room bonsai and placed outside during the summer months. It has a very attractive smooth bark, and grey and white fluffy flowers which form in clusters of three followed by white flat-ended capsules.

Position   Plenty of light, place outside on warm days.
Temperature   Cold room, with a temperature of 16°C (61°F).
Propagation   Seed sown between February and March in compost Code 1, with a temperature of 13–16°C (55–61°F), cover seed tray with propagator lid or a piece of glass.
Compost   Code 4, keep compost moist during the summer months.
Root prune   Prune every two years up to four, then every three years. Care should be taken, as roots are prone to rotting.
Pest   Mainly pest free.
Disease   Mainly free from disease.

For other eucalyptus see blue gum and lemon.

CITRON

Citron (*Citrus medica*), a small-growing tree from the Far East, can make an excellent semi-cold room indoor bonsai. The flowers,

Fig 94   Citrus, 15 years old.

which are pinkish-white and fragrant, tend to be too large for the tree. The fruits would be too heavy for the small, fine branches of a bonsai, therefore it would be better to remove the flowers once they have gone over or just before they set seed.

Position   Plenty of light.
Temperature   Between 18–21°C (64–70°F), never allow winter temperatures to fall below 13°C (55°F).
Propagation   Seed or cuttings.
Seed   Sow seeds in compost Code 1, at a temperature of 16°C (61°F).
Cuttings   Semi-ripe, with bottom heat at a temperature of 18°C (64°F).
Compost   Code 4.
Root prune   Every two years up to six, then every three years.
Pest   Red spider mite.
Disease   Mainly free from disease.

For other citrus see grapefruit, lemon, orange, seville orange, sweet orange and tangerine.

DATE PALM

An evergreen palm from Asia, date palm (*Phoenix roebelenii*) will make an excellent indoor bonsai, especially when grown in volcanic rock.

Position   Light shade and good ventilation. Keep the compost between dry and moist during the winter months, water well during the summer months.
Temperature   Never allow the temperature to drop below 13°C (55°F) during the winter months. Summer temperatures should be 18°C (64°F).
Propagation   Seed and suckers.
Seed   Sow between February and March in a compost Code 1, with a temperature between 18–21°C (64–70°F).

Suckers   Suckers can be transplanted during the month of May into individual training pots with compost Code 3 and kept at a temperature between 18–21°C (64–70°). Removing suckers is also a form of pruning, therefore no other pruning is required.
Compost   Code 3 or volcanic rock and tufa.
Root pruning   Every two years for pot grown, no root pruning when grown in rock or tufa.
Pest   Mealybugs, red spider mite.
Disease   Mainly free from disease.

DRAGON TREE

A good, evergreen indoor bonsai from the Canary Islands, dragon tree (*Dracaena draco*) is an excellent tree for the beginner, and has a very attractive root system when exposed in a flat bonsai dish. One of the longer-living trees, said to live up to 1,000 years old, a

Fig 95   Dragon tree, 5 years old.

103

well-known dragon tree is used as a show piece on one of the Canary Islands.

Position Plenty of light and good ventilation.
Temperature Winter temperature of 10°C (50°F), but will tolerate slightly lower temperatures. Summer temperatures between 16–18°C (61–64°F).
Propagation Cuttings. Most good garden centres with a houseplant section should be able to supply you with your first seedling or plant. From this take 7.5cm (3in) mature stem cuttings in April and place in a compost Code 2 on a warm bench or in a propagator at a temperature of 21°C (70°F).
Compost Code 4.
Root pruning Carefully prune the root every two years. Do not over-water for the next three weeks, stop feeding for one month.
Pest Root mealybug, red spider mite.
Disease Mainly free from disease.

FIG

The fig (*Ficus deltoidea* and *F. diversifolia*) is a small evergreen tree from India. It is commonly known as the mistletoe fig or cherry banyan and produces yellow-red fruits. A good fruiting bonsai for the beginner.

Position Plenty of light but not direct sunlight; good ventilation.
Temperature Winter temperature 10°C (50°F). Summer, 16–18°C (61–64°F).
Propagation Plant should be available from good garden centres with houseplant sections, or from cuttings and air-layering.
Cuttings Cuttings can be taken between the months of April and June. Take side shoots between 7.5–10cm (3–4in) long and place them in compost Code 2, at a temperature of 18°C (64°F).
Air-layering See propagation section on air-layering.

Fig 96   Weeping fig, 6 years old.

Compost Code 4.
Root prune Every two years. Roots can be temperamental.
Pest Scale insects.
Disease Root rot (see chapter 10).

GRAPEFRUIT

The grapefruit (*Citrus paradisi*) can be trained into a semi-cold room indoor bonsai. Flowers are white and fruits are far too large for bonsai. Therefore remove flowers before they set seed.

Position Part shade during the summer months, full light during the winter. Keep the compost moist through the summer.
Temperature Winter temperature between 7–10°C (45– 50°F), summer temperature 18°C (64°F).
Propagation Seed and cuttings.

Seed Sow seeds in March in compost Code I at a temperature of 16°C (61°F).

Cuttings Take semi-ripe cuttings 7.5–10cm (3–4in) during the months of July and August, in compost Code 2 with a bottom heat temperature of 18°C (64°F).

Compost Code 4.

Root prune Grapefruit do not like root pruning, therefore prune every three years during October or November.

Pest Mealybug.

Disease Mainly free from disease.

For other citrus see citron, lemon, orange, seville orange, sweet orange and tangerine.

JADE TREE

In past years the jade tree (*Crassula*, many forms) has been classed as a houseplant rather than a bonsai, although the Japanese

Fig 97 Jade tree, 6 years old.

have been using it for several years as an indoor bonsai. Another common name is the money tree. It is very easy to look after and an excellent tree for the beginner. However, the jade can become top-heavy if left unpruned.

Position Good light and plenty of sun.

Temperature Winter temperatures should not fall below 10°C (50°F), although jade will tolerate slightly lower temperatures. Summer temperatures between 16–18°C (61–64°F).

Propagation Very easy from leaf cuttings. During the spring remove a leaf and allow it to dry for a day or two, then pin to the surface of compost Code 2.

Compost Code 4.

Root pruning Every three years. Keep pinching back top growth.

Pest Mealybug.

Disease Mainly free from disease, but needs careful watering.

JAPANESE PAGODA TREE

A small tree from China and Korea, the Japanese pagoda tree (*Sophora japonica*) can be trained into a cold room flowering bonsai. It has white, pea-like flowers followed by long pods containing the seed.

Position Plenty of light and sun, good ventilation. Can be kept outside in a south-facing position during a warm summer, but must be kept out of strong winds.

Temperature Winter temperature of 10°C (50°F), summer temperature between 16–18°C (61–64°F).

Propagation Sow seeds during the months of March and April in compost Code 1. In a coldframe or glasshouse, no heat is required.

Compost Code 4.

Root pruning Every year up to five, then every two years.

Pest Mainly pest free.

Disease Mainly free from disease.

KOWHAI

A slow growing tree from New Zealand, *Sophora tetraptera* is also called New Zealand laburnum. Good cold room, indoor, flowering bonsai for the beginner. The flowers are yellow and followed by long pods containing seed.

Another kowhai, *Sophora microphylla* is also from New Zealand. Smaller in height than *Sophora tetraptera*, it has the same coloured flower which shows itself between the months of April and May followed by long pods containing seed.

Position Plenty of light and sun, good ventilation. Place outside in a south-facing position during warm days in the summer, but keep out of cold winds.
Temperature Winter temperature 10°C (50°F), summer between 16-18°C (61-64°F).
Propagation Sow seeds during the months of March and April in compost Code 1. In a cold frame or glasshouse, no heat is required.
Compost Code 4.
Root prune Every year up to five, then every two years.
Pest Mainly pest free.
Disease Mainly free from disease.

LEMON (Citrus limon)

A small growing tree from East Asia and less hardy than other Citrus bonsai, lemon (*Citrus limon*) should be grown in a constant warm temperature with plenty of light. The tree has fragrant flowers, followed by the fruit. The fruit would be too large for a small bonsai and can take up to one year to ripen, therefore unless grown as a large specimen bonsai I would suggest you remove the flower heads once they have gone over.

Position Full light, but not direct sunlight. Good ventilation.

Temperature Winter temperature of 10°C (50°F), summer temperature about 18°C (64°F).
Propagation Seed or cuttings.
Seed Sown in March with a compost Code 1 at a temperature of 16°C (61°F).
Cuttings Semi-ripe cuttings taken in the last two weeks of July or the first two weeks in August. Place them in a compost Code 2 with bottom heat at a temperature of 18°C (64°F).
Compost Code 4.
Root prune Lemon trees do not like root pruning, therefore prune every three years between the months of November and December. After pruning do not over-water for the next two to four weeks and do not feed for four weeks.
Pest Mealybug.
Disease Mainly free from disease.

For other citrus see citron, orange, seville orange, sweet orange.

LEMON

Now you can see why common names can become confusing. The lemon (*Eucalyptus citriodora*) is a form of eucalyptus with leaves that are scented of lemon, adding to the attractive stems and making it a prized bonsai to collect.

Position Plenty of light, place outside on warm days.
Temperature Cold room with a temperature of 16°C (61°F).
Propagation Seed sown between February to March in compost Code 1, with a temperature between 13-16°C (55-61°F).
Compost Code 4, keep moist during the summer months.
Root prune Every two years up to five, then every three years. Take care when root pruning; roots are prone to rotting.
Pest Red spider mite, mealybug.
Disease Mainly free from disease.

MONKEY PUZZLE

The monkey puzzle (*Araucaria araucana*) is an evergreen tree from Chile which will make an excellent cold room bonsai and a good bonsai for the beginner. There is also the less hardy form called the Norfolk Island pine. (*A. heterophylla*), but this does not form such a good shape as the *A. araucana*.

Position Plenty of light and good ventilation; place in a frost-free room.
Temperature Winter temperature between 5–10°C (41–50°F), summer temperature between 16–18°C (61–64°F).
Propagation Seed sown in March in compost Code 1, at a temperature of 13°C (55°F).
Compost Code 4.
Root prune Every year up to five, then every two years.
Pest Mainly pest free.
Disease Mainly free from disease.

MYRTLE

An evergreen tree from Greece, myrtle (*Myrtus communis*) can make a good cold room flowering bonsai with aromatic leaves. This bonsai begins to flower in June and flowers can last until August. The flowers are white and are followed by purple to black fruits.

Position Plenty of light and part sun, good ventilation. Keep compost moist during the summer months.
Temperature Winter temperature between 5–10°C (41–50°F), summer temperature between 16–18°C (61–64°F).
Propagation Purchase the first plant from the houseplant section of a good garden centre or bonsai nursery and use it as a stock plant to take cuttings from.
Cuttings Take non-flowering side shoots between 5–7.5cm (3–4in) in length with a heel.

Use compost Code 2 and a bottom heat temperature of 16°C (61°F).
Compost Code 4.
Root prune Every year up to five, then every two years.
Pest Mainly pest free.
Disease Mainly free from disease.

OLIVE TREE

The olive tree (*Olea*) will make a very suitable evergreen indoor coldroom bonsai, but will take several years before it starts to fruit.

Position Plenty of light, but not direct sunlight.
Temperature During the winter period temperatures should remain at 10°C (50°F), but the

Fig 98   Olive tree, 7 years old.

bonsai will tolerate slightly lower temperatures for very short periods. Summer temperatures between 16–18°C (61–64°F) should be maintained as far as possible.

Propagation Take semi-ripe cuttings in July and place in a cold frame or glasshouse. Use compost Code 2 and bottom heat with a temperature between 16–18°C (61–64°F).

Compost Code 4.

Root prune Every year up to five, then every two years.

Pest Mainly pest free.

Disease Mainly free from disease.

ORANGE

This small orange tree, *Citrus mitis*, comes from the Philippines and will make an excellent flowering indoor bonsai. If grown as a large specimen it will also make a good fruiting bonsai, but for the beginner it is best to grow as a simple flowering bonsai. The flowers are white and very fragrant, which adds to the beauty when it is grown in a conservatory.

Position Plenty of light and sun, but shade on very hot, sunny days. Needs good ventilation and a frost-free room.

Temperature Never allow the winter temperature to drop below 13°C (55°F). Summer temperature between 18–21°C (64–70°F).

Propagation Seed or cuttings.

Seed Sow seed in March in compost Code 1 at a temperature of 16°C (61°F).

Cuttings Take semi-ripe cuttings between the months of July and August. Place in compost Code 2 with a bottom heat temperature of 18°C (64°F).

Compost Code 4.

Root prune Every two years up to four, then every three years.

Pest Mealybug.

Disease Mainly free from disease.

Fig 99 Pomegranate, 8 years old, starting to flower.

POMEGRANATE

Punica granatum is an excellent small deciduous tree from Iran, suitable for indoor bonsai in either a cold or warm room. The flowers on the pomegranate are scarlet and tubular in shape, showing themselves during the months between June and September.

Another pomegranate, *Punica granatum* 'Nana' is smaller in size, flower and fruit, making it more suitable to grow as a bonsai than *P. granatum*.

Position Plenty of light and full sun, good ventilation at all times. Water well during the growing season in the summer, but keep the compost only moist during the winter.

Temperature Winter temperature can drop

to 7°C (45°F) to allow the tree to drop its foliage. Summer temperature between 18–21°C (64–70°F). Keep away from frost.

Propagation Seed and cuttings.

Seed Seeds are sown in March in compost Code 1 between a temperature of 16–18°C (61–64°F).

Cuttings Take semi-ripe cuttings with a heel between 7.5–9 cm (3–3.5in) long during the later part of July to the beginning of August, place in compost Code 2, with a bottom heat temperature of 16–18°C (61–64°F).

Compost Code 4.

Root prune Every year up to five, then every two years.

Pest Mainly pest free.

Disease Mainly free from disease.

RHODODENDRON / AZALEA

As stated before, rhododendron and azalea are closely linked and some of them, such as the large, hardy shrub and tree forms like *Rhododendron arboreum*, are best suited for outdoor conditions. There are, however, much smaller tender forms which are ideally suited for cold to warm room indoor bonsai. To write about them all would take a complete book on its own. Therefore, I have selected just a few for the beginner.

Cold Room Rhododendrons

Rhododendron indicum is a small growing evergreen to semi-evergreen shrub with flowers either red or pink. May be referred to as Indian azalea. 'Balsaminiflorum' is a dwarf, with double salmon-pink flowers. 'Kok-in-shita' is a dwarf with rose-salmon flowers.

Position Part shade, good ventilation, cold room, but frost free.

Temperature Winter temperature may drop to 10°C (50°F), summer temperature should be between 13–16°C (55–61°F).

Propagation Nursery stock, seed, cuttings, layering and grafting.

Nursery stock Most garden centres will stock a wide range of rhododendron/azalea, but finding small seedlings may be a problem.

Seed The seeds are sown between March and April; no heat is required if there is a normal start to the year, but if temperatures are low then use heat at a temperature of 13–16°C (55–61°F). See also the fine seed sowing in the seed sowing section.

Cuttings Semi-ripe cuttings taken between June and August, place in compost Code 2 with bottom heat at a temperature of 21°C (70°F). Cuttings may also be placed in a mist unit with bottom heat.

Fig 100   Indoor pine, 7 years old.

Layering Layering may be carried out any time between the beginning of April to the end of August.

Grafting Not for the beginner but if you do wish to try, read through how to saddle graft (page 31).

Compost Code 3.

Pest Caterpillars, rhododendron leafhopper, rhododendron bug, whiteflies.

Disease Chlorosis, rhododendron bud-blast, silver leaf.

SAGO PALM

The sago (*Cycas revoluta*) is grown as an artistic bonsai and could otherwise be confused with a glorified house plant. As a bonsai, the sago expresses itself best when grown over, or planted into, volcanic rock which is then placed on a flat bonsai dish without drainage holes and filled with water.

Another way of displaying the sago is in a deep pot, the same as the type used for cascade plantings. This could have artistic Japanese or Chinese markings on it.

Position Sun or part shade.

Temperature Winter temperature should never fall below 10°C (50°F). Summer temperatures between 16–18°C (61–64°F).

Propagation Seed sown between February and April in compost Code 1 with a temperature of 24°C (75°F). Use a deep seed tray or pot due to the size of the seed.

Suckers Remove suckers during April and May and place into compost Code 4.

Compost Code 4.

Root prune Every three years; may be troublesome. When grown in a rock no root pruning is required.

Pest Red spider mite.

Disease Mainly free from disease.

Fig 100(a) A 10 year old palm growing in a piece of tufa.

Fig 100(b) The growth cycle of the palm from seed (bottom centre) seedling (bottom left) seedling in bonsai pot (bottom right) to mature tree planted in tufa rock (top).

CHAPTER 10

Pests and Diseases

Bonsai trees are subject to attack from pests and diseases the same as any other tree, shrub, or houseplant. The advantages of the bonsai over the other large tree and shrub forms growing in the wild are that manual control such as removing insects by hand or moving the bonsai away from an insect-infested area are possible, thereby cutting down on the need for chemical sprays. Diseases are not so easily spotted and only tell-tale signs of yellowing leaves, unsightly marks, wilting and die-back will give some indication of the plant being diseased, but even then the visible condition may have nothing to do with a disease and may be caused through under or over watering, over or under feeding, strong sunlight, lack of light and temperatures being too high or too low.

Pests and diseases can be a very worrying subject, but in fact most bonsai are quite trouble-free, except for succumbing to the most common, such as aphids, caterpillars, mildews, rots and rusts. There are, however, a few diseases which, if not stopped in the early stages, may have effects not only on the host bonsai, but throughout your collection of bonsai. When reading through the list of insects you will see the Latin name as well as the common name; it is not important to learn the Latin name, I simply give it in case you would like to study the individual insect in more detail. The insect list shows individual forms of the same insect group, such as the aphid, which attacks one type of bonsai whilst leaving the one next to it untouched, but you will find in most cases the control and treatment is the same for the whole group.

IMPORTED TREES

Government regulations state that trees and shrubs imported from certain parts of the world cannot enter this country without first obtaining a certificate of health from the country of origin. Those from outside the European Community will need to be placed in isolation on arrival in this country and then inspected several times by qualified plant health officials from the ministry. Many first-time buyers are unaware of such rules, and when told, class them as being no more than government red tape. These rules are anything but red tape and without strict import control this country could be over-run with new strains of pest and disease which in turn will mean new forms of sprays adding to our ever increasing chemical pollution problems.

Back Door Imports

Some trees find their way into the country in shopping bags, suitcases and via black market activities. I cannot stress enough to the bonsai grower the importance of not purchasing such a tree. It may be excellent bonsai at a very reasonable price, but at the same time you are taking the risk of losing your complete bonsai collection through a pest or disease and at the same time risking serious trouble with the authorities.

HYGIENE

Hygiene plays a very important part in the control of pests and diseases. Dead leaves, off-cuts from pruning, old soil all help to increase pest and disease problems. Always burn and never compost diseased foliage or wood. Tools should be kept clean and sterilised after pruning a diseased bonsai, old pots and trays washed before using again. Old compost that has contained a diseased or pest-infested bonsai should be thrown away. Following basic hygiene rules such as these will help to control the spread of pests and disease.

CHEMICAL SPRAYS

There is a wide range of insecticides and fungicides on the modern garden centre shelves. Many are similar in content and will work as well as the next, but there are a few specially designed for a particular insect or disease. To recommend chemicals by brand name is almost impossible because testing all the sprays on the market would take so long that most of them would have been out-dated by new chemicals; to give the brand names of those I have tested would also be unfair on the rest. Therefore, the answer is first to identify the pest or disease, then to ask for advice at your local garden centre. They should be able to supply you with either a general spray that will cover most pests and diseases or one which will control your individual problem.

Mixing Sprays

Never mix two chemicals unless it states on the container which chemicals are compatible, and never follow one spray with another without first washing the spray through with clean water. Not only will mixing the wrong combination of chemicals together become toxic and dangerous to yourself, it will also damage the foliage on your bonsai and may even cause the death of the tree.

Contact and Systemic Sprays

There are two kinds of sprays; contact sprays work on the outside of the bonsai, and the systemic works on the 'inside'. The contact sticks to the surface of the foliage and kills anything which lands on it, whilst the systemic circulates in the sap of the bonsai and kills insects which feed on it. Rain can wash away the contact, and therefore they need to be sprayed more frequently, whereas the systemic is inside the bonsai and it should last longer.

Damage to the Foliage

Some bonsai, such as maples, will not tolerate chemical sprays. Scorch marks will follow chemical spraying, leaving the foliage looking unsightly and sick, and in some cases causing the leaves to fall off. One way to overcome this problem with the maple is to spray with a systemic insecticide just as the buds start to burst. This allows the chemical to enter into the bonsai sap system without damaging the foliage which is just starting to unfold, and should last up to three weeks, protecting the bonsai at the beginning of the season. This is then followed by spraying once a week with clean, soapy water, using a fairly strong jet on the spray. Basically, this control is mainly for aphids. Larger insects such as caterpillars should be removed by hand. Other insects such as woolly aphid and mealybug are removed by rubbing them off with a cotton bud impregnated with a solution of methylated spirit, as described later.

Rules to Follow

Before we move on to the individual pest and disease section, it would be advisable to read through a set of basic do's and don'ts on using chemicals:

1   Children should be supervised before and during the use of chemicals.
2   Never keep chemicals in unmarked containers. If moved to other containers, clearly mark them with the name and date when purchased.
3   Always read the instructions on the container before use, making notes of danger to eyes, etc.
4   Never mix chemicals unless stated on container.
5   Never spray on windy days or in direct sunlight.
6   Always use rubber gloves and a small face mask. If there is any sign of a headache, sore throat, eye irritation, dizzy spells or feeling sick, stop spraying immediately and consult your doctor.
7   Keep one spray container for pest and disease sprays *only*, and always wash out the container with clean water after use.
8   Try to estimate how much spray you will need. Never keep the mixture after spraying, as it may turn toxic. Always dispose of chemicals safely – do not release into water ways or drains.

Flowering and Fruiting Bonsai

Never spray your bonsai with an insecticide or fungicide during the flowering season for fear of harming helpful insects such as bees.

Chemical List

The following list is a guide to be used in conjunction with the recommendations given by the garden centre from which you purchase the chemical, but remember that the names used in the list are not brand names but chemical names. Therefore, make sure that you carefully read through and follow any instructions given by the manufacturers

before attempting to use the spray. Check the instructions for plants suitable for spraying and take notice of other warnings, such as 'Do not eat or drink when spraying'. Remember that Japanese maples (*Acer palmatum*) will not tolerate any form of insecticide spray. Those keeping fish should check if spray is harmful to fish.

Insecticides

The term for mites, such as the red spider mite, is 'Acarina', therefore an 'Acaricide' is a chemical used for the control of mites. They are usually harmful to fish.

Derris   Contact spray for aphid, caterpillars and used as an acaricide for red spider mite.
Dimethoate   Systemic, for aphid and red spider mite. Harmful to fish, bees and pets.
Gamma-HCH   Contact, smokes and sprays for the control of aphid, caterpillars and woolly aphid. Harmful to fish, bees and pets.
Malathion   Contact, used for aphid, woolly aphid, mealybug, scale insects and whiteflies, can also be used as an acaricide for red spider mite.

Fungicides

Benomyl   Systemic fungicide, used to control botrytis, powder mildew and wilts. Harmful to fish and pets, and may cause irritation to eyes, nose, throat and skin.
Captan   Sometimes used by manufacturers with HCH and used to control botrytis. Harmful to fish.
Dinocap   For the control of powder mildew, but will also help to control red spider mite. Harmful to fish.

PESTS

Ants

Other than tunnelling through the compost and forming nests, or collecting the odd small seed from the seed tray, ants do very little damage to the bonsai tree. In most cases ants are only found on bonsai when aphids are present, producing honeydew which the ants feed on.

Control Find and destroy the nest; it is often found close to the area where the host bonsai is kept. Re-pot and change compost if nest is found in pot. Follow spraying programme to control aphids on bonsai.

Aphids

There are many different forms of aphids, far too many to show in this book. Aphids are known as sap suckers, which means what it says, they feed on the sap of the bonsai's young foliage and will, therefore, cause problems not only to the foliage, but to the entire tree if a virus is transmitted by the aphid feeding on a host with a virus then moving on to a disease-free host. Several bonsai may be infected in this way in a very short space of time. Aphid-infested bonsai usually have tell-tale signs of sticky honeydew and sooty moulds covering the foliage. This will hinder the bonsai's growth as well as looking unsightly. Therefore, control of aphid breeding and movement plays an important part in the health of your bonsai.

Glasshouse Aphid (*Aulacorthum solani*) Yellow to green in colour. This aphid feeds on the young foliage of many types of indoor, coldroom and outdoor bonsai during a warm summer.

Control For bonsai other than maple and some forms of prunus, alternate spraying with contact and systemic insecticides throughout spraying programme. For maples, jet spray with soapy water once or twice a week. Smoke glasshouses to kill overwintering eggs before the start of the season. See chemical list.

Woolly Aphid (*Eriosoma lanigerum*) This brown aphid, which covers itself in a white, woolly wax, can be a serious threat to bonsai growers. It feeds on the fine, twiggy branches of several types of bonsai, especially those flowering and fruiting bonsai such as crab apple, cotoneaster and hawthorn. Branches that have been attacked may die back, or in the case of crab apple form a canker. (See die-back, page 118.)

Control Follow a spraying programme, using contact and systemic insecticide, remove by hand with cotton bud and white spirit.

Capsid Bugs

Common Green Capsid (*Lygocoris padulinus*) **Apple Capsid** (*Plesiocoris rugicollis*) Occasionally the young capsid bug may be found feeding on the new foliage and blossom of the bonsai crab apple and hawthorn. It can be recognised by its yellow to green colour.

Control Check bonsai during the winter period for signs of eggs usually found hidden away in fine, twiggy parts of the bonsai. These can be rubbed off by hand with a cotton bud covered with methylated spirit. Use a contact or systemic insecticide from the spring onwards, but not during the flowering period.

Caterpillars

As you will know, caterpillars (*Lepidoptera*) are the young (larvae) of moths and butterflies. The majority of types that attack bonsai are moths and most are controlled with the same spraying programme but, as with the aphid, there are those which will only attack certain types of bonsai and therefore I have shown the individual caterpillar and the bonsai it will attack first.

Azalea Leaf Minor (*Caloptilia azaleella*) This caterpillar will attack indoor bonsai azaleas, causing the foliage to drop and become unsightly. This small yellow to green caterpillar can be found hiding in leaves which it has pulled together by silk threads.

Control Alternate spraying with a contact and systemic before flowering and afterwards, but not whilst the bonsai is flowering.

Goat Moth (*Cossus*) Only once have I found this caterpillar, and that was on an English elm with a very thick trunk which until the time of the attack was one of my pride and joy bonsai. Unlike most caterpillars that feed on the foliage of a bonsai, this juvenile and fairly large pink to red-brown caterpillar (which will also attack ash, beech, oak and many other types of bonsai) causes its damage by tunnelling into the base of the bonsai's trunk. It is sad to say that the bonsai did not survive the attack, which made me look closely at this insect. I found that the adult lays its eggs during the night in any crooks and crannies it may find on the bonsai's trunk between the months of June and July. When the eggs containing the caterpillars hatch, the caterpillars then work their way into the trunk where they may stay for long periods, feeding on the inside of the bonsai.

Control Only when the moss was removed from the base of the trunk was the entrance to the tunnel found. Into this I sprayed a hard jet of contact insecticide, followed by a fine mist to give a fumigating effect. This killed the caterpillar, but it was too late to save the tree.

Hawthorn Webber (*Scythropia crataegella*) Both the hawthorn and the cotoneaster are attacked by this caterpillar. The first signs of this small yellow to brown and sometimes red caterpillar are when a fine silk webbing can be seen on the branch system from the spring onwards.

Control Alternate with a contact and systemic insecticide throughout your spraying programme. Remove any cocoons found and destroy them.

Juniper Webber (*Dichomeris marginella*) Bonsai juniper can be seriously affected by this caterpillar which is small and brown in colour and causes unsightly brown areas, which may finally lead to the death of the branch or complete tree.

Control Keep checking for signs of foliage turning brown, which may be caused by other problems such as windscorch, but if the caterpillar is present you will find a silk webbing. Alternate spraying with a contact and systemic insecticide throughout your spraying programme.

Oak Tortrix (*Tortrix viridana*) Termed in my evening class the 'hanging caterpillar', because of the way it hangs from the end of branches on silk threads, damage is caused by this green to grey caterpillar pulling the foliage together and then eating the leaf from the inside.

Common Tortrix Other forms of *Tortrix* may attack your bonsai tree and a good way of recognising one is to place it on the ground and touch its head which, if it is a *Tortrix*, will make a backward movement.

Control Alternate spraying with contact and systemic insecticide throughout your spraying programme. Also remove by hand and destroy any caterpillar found.

Pine Looper (*Bupalus piniaria*) I have never had a bonsai attacked by this fairly large green caterpillar and have only seen damaged trees in large forests, but it has been known to attack trees in gardens. The damage is caused by the caterpillar eating the pine needles and causing large, brown unsightly areas on the tree with the caterpillar hanging on a silk thread in a similar manner to the *Tortrix*.

Control As I have said, attacks to bonsai trees are unknown to my knowledge, but following a spraying programme with contact and systemic insecticides should give you cover against this pest.

Pine Shoot Moth(*Rhyacionia buoliana*) This very small caterpillar works its way into the buds. of the bonsai pine where it then stays during the winter months and destroys the new growth in the spring. Therefore, unlike the other caterpillars which can actually be seen, it is a case of prevention rather than cure.

Control Alternate with a contact and a systemic and carry your programme well into the latter part of the autumn and early part of the winter.

Mealybug

The mealybug (*Pseudococcus obscurus*) will attack indoor, cold room and, in very warm summers, hardy outdoor bonsai. The mealybug, which is recognised by its white-waxy covering, attacks the bonsai, weakening it and therefore rendering it unsuitable for bonsai training. Most mealybugs are found on the bonsai's branches and trunk, but on occasions they will also infest the root system.

Control Mealybug survive best in a warm temperature, therefore ventilate to keep temperatures down. Removal by hand with a cotton bud covered with methylated spirit is the best way of destroying this pest. Isolate any bonsai found with mealybug until the bonsai is completely free from the pest. Follow a spraying programme, alternating between contact and systemic insecticide.

Mites

Conifer Mite (*Oligonychus ununguis*) This mite will attack bonsai from the beginning of the year onwards causing it to turn yellow and, in some cases, drop its foliage. Juniper, pine and other conifer-type bonsai can be seriously damaged by this mite.

Control Start your spraying programme from the end of March, alternating between a contact and systemic insecticide.

Fruit Tree Red Spider (*Panonychus ulmi*) This is the main, but not the only red spider to attack your fruiting bonsai such as crab apple and peach. Many beginners, when they first come across the term 'red spider mite', automatically think of a spider such as a smaller version of the type found about the house. In fact the mite and spider are distant relatives, but other than its speed of movement, you are looking for something different in shape, as shown in Fig 101.

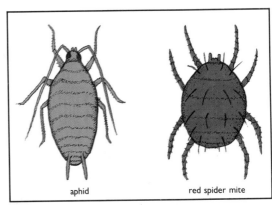

aphid   red spider mite

Fig 101   Two of the most troublesome pests, the aphid and the red spider mite.

Control Follow spraying programme using one of the chemicals for fruit red spider, under chemical control section.

Red Spider Mite/Glasshouse (*Tetranychus urticae* and *Tetranychus cinnabarinus*) These tiny mites attack many different types of indoor bonsai, covering their foliage with a very fine silk webbing which may only be noticeable by looking down or across the leaf at eye level. The foliage is weakened by the mites' attack, changes colour and dies.

Control Red spiders love hot, dry conditions, therefore ventilate to control temperatures and spray bonsai with a fine mist of clean water once daily during warm periods. A humidity tray will help, but remember not to stand the bonsai in water. Follow a spraying programme throughout the year.

Rhododendron Bug

The juvenile bug (nymphs) of *Stephanitis rhododendri* start feeding on the bonsai's foliage from the spring onwards causing the foliage to turn yellow and brown which in turn may cause it to drop.

Control Alternate spraying with a contact and systemic insecticide from the end of March onwards throughout the growing season.

DISEASES

Bonsai trees will be affected by and show the same symptoms as normal size trees growing in the wild, parklands and gardens. The bonsai should, however, be easier to control than its larger counterpart, basically because of its size (which means you do not have to climb up it to inspect the top of the tree!), and the fact that the bonsai is portable, meaning that it can be moved into special care areas.

Spotting a disease on the bonsai can be fairly easy when it is a case of recognising large swellings, colourful spots and dead branches, but foliage changing colour, wilting and so on may be misleading to the beginner. Therefore, reading about bonsai diseases will help, but only through time and experience will you fully learn these things.

Toward the back of the disease section I have talked about weather conditions such as temperature, rain, shade and strong sunlight which may affect the bonsai, and the beginner may be confused into thinking the bonsai is being attacked by a disease. The same can happen due to incorrect feeding and watering, so it is important to read through this section carefully before taking any drastic measures such as pruning or over-spraying.

Coral Spot

This fungus (*Nectria cinnabarina*) will attack almost any bonsai tree, causing die-back and in most bonsai cases, killing the tree or making drastic pruning measures necessary. Once the bonsai has been attacked by this fungus the grower lives in fear of it returning and placing other bonsai at risk. Therefore in bad cases it is probably best to destroy such a bonsai by burning. Coral spot is recognised by its salmon-pink coloured growths about the size of a pinhead.

Below is a list of rules to follow when you come across coral spot, one set of rules for prevention and the other for cure; both should be followed to the letter.

Control / Prevention

1 Hygiene is the most important factor in prevention, so never leave pruning wood lying about. Always keep a plastic bag to place the prunings in and then burn them at the first opportunity.
2 Check for old tree stumps in your garden close to the bonsai. Cut, remove and burn any

found. An old tree stump may look very nice covered with a climber or ground cover plant, but it may also cause the death of your prized bonsai by harbouring disease. At the same time, check all old wooden objects for the fungus; I have even found it on the bottom of back doors, especially old cottage-type buildings.

3 Always use fresh soil which is pest and disease free. Check the area used for mixing the soil. If there is any sign of coral spot, burn the board and find a replacement.

4 When pruning during the summer or winter-time, make sure the cuts are close to a joint and on an angle that allows water to run away from the pruning cut. (See pruning to a bud, page 44.)

5 Always clean your pruning tool with methylated or surgical spirit before use. Paint all pruning cuts with a wound sealant directly after finishing the cut.

6 Check for the disease at the start of the year especially during the spring, then use a systemic fungicide throughout the growing season.

Cure

Pruning is the best cure for this disease, but the cut is made several centimetres away from the diseased area, back into clean wood. Sometimes the pruning may be so drastic that you should consider whether it is worth keeping the bonsai at all.

Damping Off Disease

See damping off page 16.

Die-Back

Many bonsai suffer from die-back in one form or another, because the die-back may be caused through fungi and bacteria leading to forms of canker, scale insects (which also help to introduce fungi into the bonsai),

viruses, frost damage, wind, bad pruning and many more, all adding to the confusion. Therefore, as a general rule when coming across die-back, look for the cause which may not be simply on or in the diseased bonsai. Make notes and use the experience in the future; never say 'It's just one of those things that happens to plants', and remember, prevention is better than cure.

Control As a general rule to cover all die-back, remove diseased branches, cutting back into clean wood. As soon as the diseased part has been removed, cover the wound with a sealant containing a fungicide. Never keep the prunings; burn them or place them into a plastic bag until such a time as burning is convenient (this should be no longer than a week). Follow a spraying programme using a fungicide throughout the growing season.

Rots/Grey Mould

This disease (*Botrytis cinerea*) usually follows damping-off disease found with bonsai seedlings (see page 16); it will attack buds and cause die-back on woody sections of some coldroom bonsai. The disease is recognised by its grey, fluffy mould growing on the affected area.

Control Avoid over-watering, especially when temperatures are low, and allow for free drainage on seed trays and pots. Space seed trays and bonsai to allow light and air to circulate freely. Prune bonsai, taking out crossing branches (this allows air to travel freely through the fine branch work). Add copper fungicide to the watering programme for seedlings and spray with a fungicide throughout the growing season.

Weather Conditions

Weather conditions obviously affect outdoor hardy bonsai more than indoor bonsai. However, it is beneficial for indoor bonsai to be placed outside during a warm summer, and therefore temperature factors such as light and rain must all be taken into consideration by indoor bonsai growers.

Light

The light factor, during the growing season, is the most important ingredient in successfully growing bonsai, even more so than temperature. I say this because the bonsai will tolerate a much wider temperature range, but the light factor needs to be kept at a constantly high level. The beginner must not confuse a high level of light with strong sunlight; in fact most bonsai prefer filtered light, hence the use of bonsai shadery. Most garden centres sell small light meters and I would advise the beginner to invest in one before siting a bonsai. Bonsai which are kept in poor light conditions show signs of leggy growth on their stems between one set of leaves and the next, and leaves turn yellow because the development of chlorophyll is restricted.

Rain

Water is a very important factor in the life of the bonsai. Rain water is far superior to tap water and should be collected wherever possible. However, too much rain water flooding the bonsai pot will cause the compost to become compacted, stopping the vital flow of air and blocking the passages between the soil particles. If this happens, the air will become stale and the moisture round the particles will become toxic, leading to poor root growth, rotting roots and in some cases the death of the tree.

Fig 102   During a wet period place a brick under the end of the pot, as shown, to assist drainage.

Control   During wet months, which can be any time of the year, it is important that the pot maintains its free-draining ability. To ensure you assist the pot's drainage, follow the basic rule of using gravel at the bottom of the pot and sharp sand in the compost. In very wet months, prop up one end of the pot to help the excess water to drain away.

Temperature

Next to light, temperature is the second most important ingredient in creating a healthy bonsai tree. Temperature controls the period of dormancy on the deciduous bonsai and many problems such as poor growth, leggy growth and dull-coloured foliage are caused when the deciduous indoor bonsai is kept at a constant temperature level throughout the year. One reason for these problems is that the bonsai cannot take the rest period it needs. Nature has built in a mechanism telling the bonsai to close down its manufacturing process to survive during certain conditions. When these conditions fail to develop, the balance of the bonsai is thrown into confusion. The same also applies to the hardy outdoor bonsai forced to keep its foliage throughout the winter.

Too high a temperature can be just as damaging as a low temperature. Problems such as heat canker will arise from high temperatures. The temperature requirements of bonsai are as follows:

Indoor bonsai The indoor bonsai are both evergreen and deciduous, tropical and subtropical, trees and shrubs. They need a totally frost-free growing environment with a temperature range between 15–21°C (59–70°C).

Coldroom bonsai Evergreen bonsai may be kept between 10–16°C (50–61°F), but the temperature should be allowed to fall to 4°C (39°F).

Less hardy bonsai Bonsai such as osmanthus, osmarea, ginkgo and Trident maple all need extra attention during the colder parts of the autumn and winter.

Hardy bonsai Bonsai such as hawthorn, elm, oak and horse chestnut will tolerate very low temperatures, but because of the pot and small amounts of soil, these bonsai will not tolerate as extreme weather conditions as their fully-grown counterparts would growing in the wild.

Fig 102(a)   An indoor tree which has been damaged by having been placed on top of a television set. Because of the extra heat red spider mite has taken a firm hold.

Fig 102(b)   A Serissa which has been placed in the wrong position. Note the black leaves caused by lack of light.

CHAPTER 11

Monthly Guide

JANUARY

Hardy Bonsai

Trees will not need as much light as during the growing season, basically because there are no leaves to photosynthesise. Therefore, problems of shelter do not create such a problem as a tree in full foliage (a shed with windows and good ventilation would suffice).

Snow

Remove snow from branches which are over-wintering in the soil outside.

Rain

For bonsai kept in a sheltered spot outside, place a brick or piece of wood under one end of the pot to help drain away excess rain-water during a heavy rain storm.

Watering

Only water to stop the tree's soil from drying out; never allow the soil to become water-logged which would in turn freeze to a solid block of ice during the low temperatures of this month.

If you are using a cold frame with heated cables for over-wintering, or a warm bench of a glasshouse, you should lift the pot and if it feels light, there is a good chance that the compost has dried out at the bottom. For those who wish to be scientifically minded, weigh the bonsai with its pot when fully watered and again before it becomes too dry. This will give you a more accurate indication of the compost condition. Under these conditions, try to keep the pot slightly moist.

Feeding

Do not feed the tree this month otherwise damage can be caused to the root system by a build-up of unused fertilisers becoming toxic.

Pests

Deciduous bonsai are usually pest-free except for those pests using your bonsai as a host plant to over-winter. Check the tree using a magnifying glass, looking in all the nooks and crannies, and remove any pests found by hand. At your local garden centre there are 'winter sprays' or 'winter washes' to kill over-wintering pests. However, these were developed for large fruit trees and I would therefore strongly recommend that you do not use them on your bonsai.

Diseases

Look out for diseases such as coral spot, rots and mould. For coral spot and rots, prune back to clean wood.

Indoor Bonsai

As outdoor temperatures drop, indoor temperatures are raised by turning up the central heating. Warm air gas central heating presents itself as the major problem, creating a warm, dry atmosphere around the surface and aerial parts of the indoor bonsai. To overcome this, a constant check on watering, keeping the compost moist but not waterlogged, is an important factor at this time of the year. Spraying the foliage of the bonsai with a fine mist spray will help to overcome the problem of dry atmosphere. Humidity trays, and dishes without holes which hold water as shown in previous chapters, can be used providing you follow the important rule of never allowing the base of the pot to be submerged in water for lengthy periods of time. Therefore, fill the tray with pebbles or use four small stones as pillars to stand the pot on, which allows water to drain through the holes in the bottom of the pot and air to enter.

Other forms of heating do not cause as many problems as the above-mentioned heating. The exception to this is a coal fire, and unless good ventilation and a dust-free atmosphere can be created, I would advise that the bonsai be kept in a well lit, ventilated corner away from the fire or in another room.

Feeding

Continue to follow a feeding programme during this month but remember to alternate between a balanced fertiliser containing N.P.K. and trace elements, and a tomato feed, also containing some trace elements. Again, the important rule is not to over feed the bonsai.

Pests

Keep a check on your bonsai for pests, looking at the underside of the leaves and in the crowded areas of the branch work. As far as possible, remove any pests found by hand. If insecticide sprays are used, remember to use a bottle type rather than an aerosol, as they will give you more control of the strength of the spray. It would be advisable to spray out of doors on a still day, but not in bright sunlight and remember to wash the container and your hands after spraying.

Diseases

The bonsai should be mainly trouble-free this time of year, except for problems caused by bad pruning, lack of light, poor ventilation, too low or too high a temperature, over watering, under watering and over feeding. These symptoms show themselves as follows:

1   Bad pruning – die-back and rots.
2   Lack of light – black growing tips.
3   Poor ventilation – general unhealthy look.
4   Temperature/watering – mildews, wilting and rots.
5   Over-feeding – wilting or too much sappy growth.

FEBRUARY

Hardy Bonsai

This month can be as cold, if not more so, than January. Therefore follow the same procedures for hardy bonsai in relation to weather, placement, pruning, watering, feeding, pests and diseases.

Planning for March

February is an excellent month when there is little going on in the hardy bonsai section, giving you time to plan your coming year's root pruning which may start from March onwards.

Pots

Choose sizes, colours and shapes to balance up with the trees that will need re-potting.

Equipment

Look at tools and sprays that need cleaning and maintenance. Decide how many seeds are to be sown this year and start to prepare your seed trays either by buying new or washing and sterilising old ones.

Pruning

Now is the time to check for frost damage in those hardy trees kept outside without heat in a cold frame or buried in the soil. If large branch work has been affected, mark ready for pruning back to clean wood at the beginning of March. Smaller branches can be marked ready for the end of March.

Soil

Check with your local garden centre to see when fresh supplies for making your compost will be available and if this is by the end of the month, preparations can be made ready for mixing during the first two weeks of March.

Pests

Hardy bonsai are usually trouble free at this time of year. Now is the time to buy your supply of chemicals; the type and quantity should have been decided when working through your spraying programme. Again, make sure that the chemicals are fresh and suited to the type of spraying you wish to perform. One important safety rule to remember is always to leave the chemical in its original bottle. Never be tempted to transfer to unmarked jars or milk bottles, or to accept any left-overs from friends or neighbours. Check for signs of attack from birds such as the bullfinch and cover bonsai with netting if necessary.

Diseases

Wilts, die-back and frost damage may be a problem this month.

Hardy seed sowing

Visit your local garden centre and look through their seeds and their suppliers' catalogue for your hardy bonsai seeds. In most cases, you will probably need to ask the garden centre to place a special order, or write direct to the suppliers yourself.

Indoor Bonsai

Keep a check on watering, and spray over the foliage if the bonsai lives in a dry atmosphere. Refer to the list on indoor bonsai (chapter 9) for the recommended winter temperatures.

Seed

Start looking for suppliers of indoor bonsai seed. Unlike the hardy seed which can often be purchased at a garden centre or easily ordered, you may have to contact a seed specialist or bonsai nursery and place your order of indoor tree seeds ready for the start of the sowing season over the next couple of months. Check seed list for placement and germination temperatures.

Feeding

Continue to follow your feeding programme, which should still contain a low nitrogen content.

Pests and Diseases

Check for pests and remove by hand if possible, otherwise spray for any disease problems. Some of the disease problems may be caused through too high or too low a temperature and bad ventilation. Therefore, again check the temperature around the tree and make sure there is adequate ventilation. Purchase new stocks of insecticide and fungicide sprays ready for the coming season.

Root Pruning and Re-potting

Decide whether your tree will need root pruning and re-potting during the next two months; if so choose your pot accordingly. It will be advisable, if root pruning and re-potting, to choose a pot either the same size or slightly larger, and never to over-pot (i.e. using a pot several times larger than the root ball). Once you have root pruned and re-potted keep the watering to a minimum over the next three weeks and do not feed for four weeks.

MARCH

Hardy bonsai

Root pruning and re-potting should be done this month. The days are beginning to lengthen, temperatures are rising and the buds will start to swell. However, frost and low temperatures can still be a problem.

Root Pruning and Re-potting

This is the best month for pruning most of your hardy bonsai, but again rather than setting a time you should be governed by the movement of the buds. Therefore, as with the feeding, if there is a forecast of further frosts, hold back until the tree shows signs of movement. If weather conditions permit, root pruning should go ahead. After the root pruning, the four most important rules to follow are:

1　Do not over-water.
2　Do not feed for three to four weeks.
3　Keep out of frost.
4　Shelter from strong winds.

As previously mentioned, if rainfall is heavy this month, place a brick or piece of wood under one end of the pot to allow excess water to drain away. On no account should you force your hardy bonsai after root pruning by placing it on a warm bench, as this could expose the damaged root system to a sudden change in temperature.

Pruning

All large branch pruning should have been carried out by this time.

Pests and Diseases

At the end of the month, spray with a systemic insecticide and fungicide. Spray all maples with a systemic insecticide just before bud burst. Care should be taken with insecticide sprays after this time, especially with this species (see page 112). Look for signs of caterpillars.

Wind

Trees kept outside growing in the soil should be sheltered from strong winds by using hessian or plastic wind-breaks.

Rain

For trees kept outside in sheltered positions, place a small stone or piece of wood under one end of the pot to help drain away excess water.

Snow

Remove any snow from branches of trees over-wintering in the soil outside.

Feeding

Start feeding and follow a feeding programme making sure you keep a notebook recording when you fed your tree and the type of feed given.

Wiring

Start wiring trees where needed.

Indoor bonsai

Watering

Depending on the type of tree, the general rule is to increase watering.

Feeding

Stop using the tomato feed and use only the balanced N.P.K. feed plus trace elements.

Pests and Diseases

Aphids, red spider mite, powdery mildew are all a danger in March. Follow a spraying programme.

APRIL

Hardy bonsai

Keep the tree out of strong winds, and do not allow the soil to dry out. If there is a heavy rainfall this month, tilt pot as shown before.

Feeding

Start feeding with a balanced N.P.K.

Pests

Aphids, mealybug and caterpillars start showing themselves. Commence a spraying programme and remove what you can by hand. Avoid spraying close to maples which may cause marking on the foliage, spraying maples instead with clean, soapy water.

Indoor bonsai

Root pruning should be completed by the end of the month. Feeding, watering and general care is the same as for March.

MAY

Hardy bonsai

Night frost can still be a problem. The tree should now be in active growth; keep a check on top and side growth.

Watering

Check watering; do not let the soil dry out and do not water when sun is on the foliage (try to water before 10am or after 5pm). If there is heavy rainfall this month, tilt pot as shown before.

Fig 103   Monkey Puzzle, 7 years old.

Fig 104 *Needle Juniper, 7 years old, planted next to a rock.*

Feeding

Feed with a tomato feed on flowering and fruiting trees, and with a general balanced N.P.K. feed on all other trees.

Holidays

From May up until the end of September, watering is one of the top priorities of bonsai growing. To allow the bonsai to dry out will in most cases cause the death of the tree, therefore it is important that arrangements are made for watering your bonsai whilst you are away.

JUNE

Hardy Bonsai

General care is the same as for May. On fruiting bonsai such as crab apple, pinch back to two buds above the fruit. This will allow more light to reach the fruit and in addition,

help to form spurs which will produce more fruit the following year.

Watering

As for May plus spraying overhead during the evening on warm days.

Pests and Diseases

Keep checking for pest and disease.

Pruning

Prune new growth.

Holiday Period

See May section on holidays.

Cuttings / Semi-ripe

See cutting section.

Indoor Bonsai

As for May.

JULY

As for June, but change feed to N.P.K. 10:14:19.

Holiday Period

See May note on holidays.

Cuttings / Semi-Ripe

See cutting section.

AUGUST

As for July. Check wiring.

Autumn Frost

Towards the end of the month keep a check on the weather conditions; if a frost is forecast then take precautions, starting with the less hardy bonsai first.

Holiday Period

See May note on holidays.

SEPTEMBER AND OCTOBER

The leaves on deciduous trees will start to show autumn colour. This time of year may be frightening to the beginner and I would therefore advise you to read through the pest and disease section on weather conditions (page 119). Remove wire during October.

Feeding

Change to a tomato feed at the beginning of September. Stop feeding at the end of October.

NOVEMBER AND DECEMBER

As for September and October. Start moving tree into its winter position. Remove dead leaves from tree, surface of pot and surrounding area. Cut back on watering.

Cuttings / Hardwood

This is the time of year for the propagation of willows, cornus and many others. The controlling factors to remember are good drainage, away from frost pockets, out of strong winds and clear of heavy shade.

Fig 105   A small cotoneaster. Feeding with a tomato feed from autumn onwards will help to ripen the berries which are produced.

Indoor Bonsai

Cut back on watering, change to a tomato feed. As far as possible try to keep the room temperature between 10–16°C (50–61°F). Cut back on water, but never allow the compost to dry out. Give the bonsai as much light as possible, but if positioned in a window, move the bonsai to a warmer spot during the night.

Pomegranate and other Indoor Deciduous Trees.

Allow the foliage to drop and the tree to enter its dormant state; this can be accomplished by placing the pomegranate into an area with a temperature just below 10°C (50°F).

Index